LONDON BRIDGE
IN AMERICA

The Bus We Loved: London's Affair with the Routemaster

The Long Player Goodbye: The Album from Vinyl to iPod and Back Again

Wish You Were Here: England on Sea

LONDON BRIDGE IN AMERICA

THE TALL STORY OF A TRANSATLANTIC CROSSING

TRAVIS ELBOROUGH

JONATHAN CAPE

LONDON

Published by Jonathan Cape 2013

2 4 6 8 10 9 7 5 3 1

Copyright © Travis Elborough 2013

Travis Elborough has asserted his right
and Patents Act 1988 to be identified as

First published in Great Britain in 2013 by
Jonathan Cape
Random House, 20 Vauxhall Bridge Road,
London SW1V 2SA

www.vintage-books.co.uk

Addresses for companies within The Random House Group Limited can be found at:
www.randomhouse.co.uk/offices.htm

The Random House Group Limited Reg. No. 954009

A CIP catalogue record for this book
is available from the British Library

ISBN 9780224096256

The Random House Group Limited supports The Forest Stewardship Council® (FSC®),
the leading international forest certification organisation. Our books carrying the FSC label
are printed on FSC® certified paper. FSC is the only forest certification scheme supported by
the leading environmental organisations, including Greenpeace. Our paper
procurement policy can be found at www.randomhouse.co.uk/environment

Typeset in Fournier MT by Palimpsest Book Production Limited,
Falkirk, Stirlingshire

Printed and bound in Great Britain by
MPG Books Group Ltd, Bodmin, Cornwall

for
David and Sydneyann Shook
and Richard Boon

CONTENTS

'If it was a question of an Imperium, he said to himself, and if one wished, as a Roman, to recover a little of the sense of that, the place to do so was on London Bridge.'

Henry James, *The Golden Bowl*

'This is the West, sir. When the legend becomes fact, print the legend.'

The Man Who Shot Liberty Valance

INTRODUCTION

Like a Rolling Stone

On 23 September 1968, the McCulloch Oil Corporation invited members of the world's press to attend a rather unusual ceremony in Lake Havasu City, Arizona – the purpose-built city it had founded in the desert just five years earlier. In the intervening period, many a journalist, eager young cub reporters and grizzled fedora-wearers alike, had been flown out to Lake Havasu City to enthuse over the landscaping of its freshly laid Civic Center Park. Or marvel at the luxuriousness of the suites in the brand new Nautical Inn Hotel. Or commend its fully stocked bar and state-of-the-art water-sporting facilities. All expenses paid, naturally.

But today was quite different.

Far from being asked to salute the up to date, the throngs of photographers, television crews and newspapermen who gathered here were expected to admire the arrival of a foundation stone from a granite bridge that was over 130 years old. A bridge deemed so arcane by its original owners in England, the City of London, that it was consequently surplus to their requirements.

What could Robert P. McCulloch, the multimillionaire oil baron and chainsaw-manufacturing king, possibly want with this old junk? First catching sight of him standing beside a tall gentleman with what looked like a badger on his head and wearing, in the 90-degree heat, a long black robe trimmed with gold, a lace ruff, knickerbocker breeches and a pair of snowy white gloves, it wasn't hard to imagine he'd succumbed to some occult sect. An impression further enhanced by the appearance of a small party of Apache Indians. Decked out in deerskins, beads and ornate feathered headdresses and carrying drums and shaking sticks, they launched into a tribal dance, whooping and chanting as they spun around, to the evident delight of the figure in the black robes – now formally introduced to the crowd as Sir Gilbert Inglefield, 'the lord mayor of London Town'.

When the dance was over, Sir Gilbert gave a short speech and presented McCulloch with a small green bottle full of a brackish-looking liquid; water, he explained, from the River Thames. And then beneath a trio of flags – the state of Arizona pennant, the Stars and Stripes and the Union Jack – with a crank of a winch handle and to rapturous applause, a stone that had travelled over

4,000 miles by ship from the Surrey Docks in Rotherhithe to Long Beach, California, and a further 300 miles by road from there to Lake Havasu, was slowly lowered into place.

The first piece of London Bridge had fallen down in America.

Its new home, as some of the less charitable souls imbibing complimentary martinis in the bar later couldn't help but observe, was a conspicuously dry, not to say outright dusty, plot of land. Work on a channel over which this famous span was destined to arch, it emerged, was yet to begin – the water was only to be diverted from the lake when the bridge itself had been completed, and 10,000 tons' worth of granite blocks reassembled piece by piece. And that arduous task was set to take another three years.

* * *

London Bridge, we were told, was in America. The 'real London Bridge', that was. Mrs Sergeant, a teacher who sported floor-length burlap skirts and long, lank centre-parted hair and rarely passed up an opportunity to whip her acoustic guitar out in lessons, was quite explicit about that. It was morning assembly and we'd just finished singing the – *that* – nursery rhyme. Yes, London Bridge, the real one, she had said quite blithely while fiddling with her capo, was now in America. To a curious child – in every sense of the word – at a primary school on the south coast of England in the mid-1970s this seemed outrageous. The real London Bridge in America? She might as well have said the moon. I'd been to London. Once. Its name also topped the odd local road sign, which always made it seem a possible, and therefore eminently plausible, destination to me, in line with, say, Brighton or Chichester nearby. America, on the other hand, was like outer space. It was something you only ever saw on television. In fact, with a handful of exceptions, most of the aliens beamed into our living room spoke with American accents.

And who had landed on the moon? Americans, surely?

America was a planet of wide-open spaces and vast gleaming cities inhabited by a tall, bronzed people gifted with immaculately coiffed hair who drove monstrous cars, all leering chrome grilles, aluminium siding and wood panelling. When not shooting each other with big, silvery guns, they appeared endlessly tasked with placing massive, handle-less brown paper bags full of food on to kitchen surfaces. Or withdrawing oversized milk cartons (were they? they definitely weren't bottles) from fridges the size of garden sheds.

A great-uncle had emigrated to California following the Second World War. For all the contact the family had with him after that, he could have died in the Blitz like his younger sister. The odd birthday card. A letter now and again with a photograph of some corn-fed second or third cousins we never expected to meet. A telephone call one Christmas. What with the static, the relatives clustering around the receiver chipping in questions, and the sheer disjointed brevity of the responses, this felt like a seance. Certainly the voice that emanated from the phone, an echoey baritone with an accent that hovered between native Redhill and adopted San Francisco, sounded like a ghost's.

Aged five, I vowed to go to America when I grew up. Much as back then I vowed to go to Mars.

When I finally went to the States as an A-level politics student in my late teens, the shopping malls, drive-through burger joints, bars, multiple television and radio stations, trucks – and their fridges – remained exhilaratingly, enchantingly other. A branch of Gap was a novelty and Rolling Rock beer a completely unknown quantity.

Typing these words in London over twenty years on, I can only reflect on how radically things changed. The increased reach and power of global brands and multinational corporations and the arrival of the Internet have all conspired to whittle away at national differences as never before. From the laptop I am using now, it is as simple to stream NPR as BBC Radio 4, watch *America's Next Top Model* as *Britain's Got Talent*, and as easy to read the *New York Times* as *The Times* of London.

I am married to an American and we visit the States about twice a year. Yet Facebook updates and online Flickr photo albums mean I sometimes feel I have a far more intimate idea of my in-laws' daily lives in Indianapolis and Richmond, Virginia, than my own less Web-savvy parents' fifty miles down the road. Though since both sets of parents have houses in the suburbs, depend on their cars to get anywhere and do nearly all of their shopping in large out-of-town retail parks, their lives oddly appear to possess greater similarities to each other, than to us in London.

In her memoir *Dear London*, the New Jersey-born writer Irma Kurtz maintained that when she first came to the British capital in

1963, it 'was less like an American city' than any she'd known. To her the whole town reeked of 'wet wool and river mud, coal smoke, boiled cabbage', and almost everything, from turning a gas fire on in a bedsit to obtaining a refill of a cup of execrable coffee in a café, seemed to require a steady outlay of heavy copper coins.

Close to fifty years later, the streets of London are paved with coffee shops and a greenhorn is likely to encounter the same international lingua perfuma of Issey Miyake, fried chicken and Krispy Kreme donuts on Tottenham Court Road as they might find on 7th Avenue. Topshop has a branch in New York. Abercrombie and Fitch two in London. And so it goes on.

Nevertheless our backdrop here, with a good deal of backstory from centuries past (and we must begin in the mists of the capital's known history), is the late 1960s – a time when each country was still capable of appearing substantially much more exotic to the other. This was a period of quite unprecedented stateside Anglophilia. London was considered 'swinging' by *Time* magazine. And American enthusiasm for a land of hope and glory that was part Princess Margaret and part the Dave Clark Five – regal yet rocking, say, historically classy but perceived to be less class-bound – was at its zenith. Conversely, British politicians and leading architects found inspiration in the thrusting modernity they saw gleaming across the Atlantic, and it was this that precipitated their desire to redevelop London into a modern car-friendly metropolis along American lines – the initiative that led the City Corporation to replace Rennie's 1831 London Bridge with a new span in the first place.

These plans, if completed, would have resulted in The Strand becoming a dual carriageway and Covent Garden being obliterated by a motorway and rows of glittering office blocks. Indeed, their New London Bridge, standing to this day, would have more in common with the Westway (London's new motorway opened in 1970) than its classical predecessor. In the Corporation's vision, Los Angeles or New Jersey, rather than Jerusalem, was to be built on the capital's grey and bomb-scarred land.

And yet for all these Utopian schemes – and it's worth noting that Thomas More, whose severed head wound up on a spike on London Bridge, placed his original Utopia somewhere near America – the late sixties was also an era of increasing anxiety about the future, when for some the past, or a partially imagined version of it, only grew more appealing. In the year of London Bridge's sale, Enoch Powell made his odious rivers of blood speech, Richard Nixon entered the White House, Martin Luther King was assassinated and protests raged about the Vietnam War on both sides of the Atlantic. Amid all this turmoil, Hollywood gave the Oscar for Best Picture that year to *Oliver!*, the all-singing-dancing version of Charles Dickens' tale of Cockney wallet-swipers. These were, as they say, interesting times.

Bridges are liminal structures. They lie between two banks, suspended over water, and for the suicidal (or the unfortunate victims of the KGB's poisoned umbrella stings) between life and death itself. That potency and their metaphorical potential have never been lost on artists, poets, novelists and harmonic vocal folk duos with choppy liquids on their minds. Accordingly, this book is really an attempt to examine what this story tells us about the Old World and the New one, England and America, then and now. As much about artifice as architecture, and lies as landscape, what follows is perhaps as serpentine as the Thames, with many loops and eddies, and possibly some high and low tides. But then a bridge crossing two continents is rather a wayward thing to span.

PART ONE

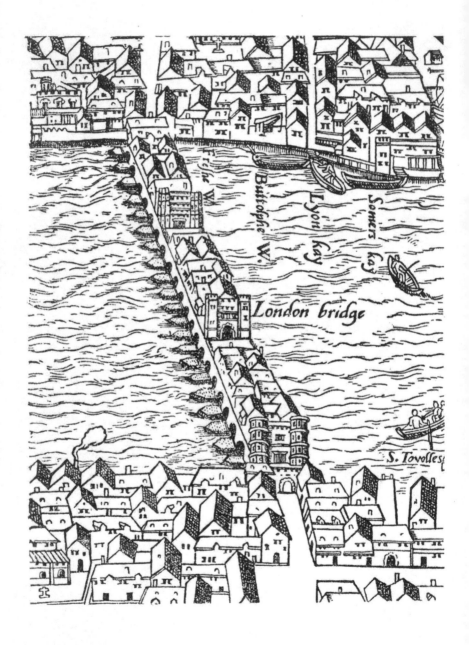

CHAPTER I

Mind the Gap

London Bridge has always been a structure that is as mythic as monumental, with its precise origins still remaining decidedly, and appropriately perhaps, foggy. The oldest written documentary proof for the existence of a river crossing at Southwark hails from a Saxon record of a witch trial. The bridge is mentioned, almost in passing, as the site of a witch's execution, with the unfortunate spell-maker being thrown off it and drowned.

But London Bridge is certainly older than that. For instance, the Romans constructed some kind of bridge in the vicinity when they first conquered Britain in AD 43. In his chronicle of the invasion campaign, the historian Dio Cassius describes the Roman commander Aulus Plautius and his troops, having landed on the Kent coast, advancing in pursuit of fleeing local tribesmen to 'the river Thames at a point near where it emptied into the ocean and at flood-tide forms a lake'. He writes that the Britons, knowing the terrain, initially evaded their pursuers by crossing the river on an area of firm ground. While some Romans actually swam after them, others used 'a bridge a little way upstream' to get over the water, 'after which they assailed the barbarians from several sides at once and cut down many of them'.

Cassius was writing 180 years after the event, and his description is vague enough to place this 'bridge', most likely an age-old ford or a hastily whipped-together military pontoon rather than a bridge per se, at either Westminster, Brentford, Battersea or Fulham. Informed opinion generally tends to favour Westminster. But the ground at Westminster, then an isle irrigated by both the Thames and the River Tyburn, was extremely marshy. And having subdued the natives, temporarily anyway, the Romans would look elsewhere for a suitable location to establish a settlement on the Thames estuary, one that could consolidate their hold in the region and eventually connect to roads to their eastern capital Colchester and its northern twin St Albans. They found the perfect spot on the upper side of the river on the high ground between Cornhill and Ludgate Hill. Above the sodden flood-plain, but served by the freshwater Fleet and Walbrook, the Thames here was also narrow enough for the construction of a strategically essential wooden bridge, probably at about twenty feet downstream of the present London Bridge, and reaching over to a gravel ledge at their 'southern defensive works' in the largely boggy Southwark.

What became of this London Bridge, eventually a solid timber fixture with a drawbridge by about AD 120, following the Romans' departure 290 years later is not known. Until the conquering Saxons reoccupied the ancient city walls in the ninth century (largely to defend themselves against incessant Viking raids) it would appear that they lived further west along the river by the Strand, and probably left Londinium and the wooden London Bridge to rot in the interim. But by the tenth century, a Saxon bridge, even if acclaimed mostly as a convenient means to dispatch witches to their deaths, starts to make more regular appearances in contemporary records. Toll rates for boats passing under the bridge – a halfpenny for a small craft with fish, a penny for a larger vessel – were listed in King Æthelred's London Laws of around 978.

And Æthelred was at the heart of one of the most legendary incidents concerning London Bridge. Known as the Unready, or ill-counselled, for his poor judgement and weak rule, he was forced into exile in Normandy, when the Danish king Svein Forkbeard and his son, Canute, or Cnut, conquered England in 1014. Svein died shortly after this, plunging the kingdom into one of those periods of regal chaos typically settled in this era by pan-Scandinavian pow-wows, invasions and/or massacres. Æthelred, seemingly invited to return by Englishmen suffering under the yoke of Cnut, then opted to forge an alliance with a former enemy, the Norwegian ruler Olaf Haraldsson, to regain control of the country.

Folklore and the Norse sagas have King Olaf sailing up the Thames to confront the Danish forces in London. He found Cnut's troops stationed on either side of the river. They had also taken up position on one of the city's bridges, described in Snorri Sturluson's Olaf Sagas as 'so broad that two wagons could pass each other upon it'. The Norwegian is alleged to have responded by rowing up to the bridge, tying ropes around its supporting piles and pulling them away, thereby plunging the Danes into the water.

Olaf's victory was celebrated in a poem by the Norse bard Ottar Svarte, a poem which is often taken to provide the origins of that famous London Bridge nursery rhyme. His verse epic, at least in

some versions – and typically there are some variations and many
doubts about its precise antiquity – begins:

> London Bridge is broken down.
>
> Gold is won, and bright renown.
>
> Shields resounding,
>
> War-horns sounding,
>
> Hild is shouting in the din!
>
> Arrows singing,
>
> Mail-coats ringing –
>
> Odin makes our Olaf win!

However, since the poem was apparently composed on pain of death,
and subject to Olaf's approval, some experts suggest the magnitude
of his assault on the bridge was quite possibly exaggerated.*

Two years later, Cnut would regain London by sailing around
the (rebuilt) timber bridge, using a ditch dug through the marshes
of Lambeth. The bridge was similarly circumvented by William
the Conqueror, who during the Norman Conquest chose to cross
the Thames at Wallingford in Oxfordshire instead. However, the
wooden bridge had a tumultuous hundred years ahead – it was
carried away in a flood in 1091, only for the rebuilt structure to
be consumed by a fire in 1136. The last wooden London Bridge

---

* Although until the remains of a Viking settlement in L'Anse aux Meadows
in Newfoundland were discovered in 1960, accounts of bands of hardy
Norsemen sailing to what sounded uncannily like North America in the likes
of Erik the Red's *Saga* were dismissed as scholarly exaggeration. So . . .

was to be completed in elm in 1163, at which point the priest who'd overseen the work, Peter de Colechurch of St Mary Colechurch in Cheapside, petitioned to build a replacement in stone.

Most likely spurred on by the examples of arches in Islamic architecture encountered on the Crusades and pilgrimages to the Holy Land, the concept of building bridges as an act of piety had come into its own in Europe by the twelfth century. An order of Benedictine monks, the Fratres Pontices (or Frères Pontifs, Brothers of the Bridge), dedicated to building bridges and providing hostels for pilgrims and travellers was first founded in Italy, but became especially widespread in France. Revered for their great hospice in Paris and their charitable deeds throughout the country, one of the best examples of their constructions was the twenty-arch masonry bridge at Avignon in Provence. Its master builder, Bénézet, a former shepherd who claimed God had personally instructed him to erect a bridge over the River Rhône, was canonised for his good works and subsequently buried in a chapel on the bridge.* While less active in Britain, their example was followed by many local abbeys and religious houses in England during the medieval period, with bridges built and maintained using donations, Church funds, tolls, and alms collected at chapels incorporated into their crossings.

Peter de Colechurch, and his successors, would do their utmost to encourage Londoners to donate land and money 'to God and the

---

* Like London Bridge it is this bridge's subsequent decay that is commemorated in a ditty – with the French school song 'Sur le pont d'Avignon' recording that half the bridge has fallen down.

Bridge'. In the very long term, their panhandling efforts paid off. By 1968 the Bridge House Estates were able to fund the rebuilding of London Bridge themselves and, having amassed an impressive portfolio of properties over the centuries, its assets are currently estimated to run to several hundred million pounds. Back in 1176 when the first stone was laid (or more likely a supporting timber pile hammered in), levying a tax on wool, along with contributions from King Henry II, Richard of Dover (the Archbishop of Canterbury) and the Pope's legate, Cardinal Hugo di Petraleone, had been necessary just to get the thing off the ground.

Comprised of nineteen irregular pointed Gothic arches of differing widths, and a drawbridge, Old London Bridge was not far off an American idea of English dentistry rendered in masonry. And its cutwaters were rather like the teeth on a plankton-skimming whale, braking the river's flow and producing a drop in water levels of up to six feet.

The bridge took thirty-three years to complete and it is estimated that as many as 200 men were killed during its construction; the majority would simply have drowned in the Thames, with fatal blows from falling masonry and malfunctioning winches, badly aimed chisels and hammers most likely accounting for the others. Peter de Colechurch, while not one of the on-site fatalities, died just four years before it was finished. His body, though, was laid to rest in a chapel on the bridge dedicated to the martyred Thomas Becket, who had been christened in the priest–builder's Cheapside church as a child. Many pilgrims, like those Chaucer later imagined at the Tabard in Southwark, had to pass over the bridge on their way to Canterbury, and were no doubt expected to be a sure touch for alms.

Along with the chapel, the bridge was intended to be fully inhabited from the start, its surface lined with two rows of tall wooden buildings, serving as workrooms, houses and shops. Walking over the bridge was little different to negotiating any crowded medieval street, though since any rubbish could be thrown into the Thames, it was probably rather cleaner than the rest of London's messy thoroughfares. And for several centuries of its 622-year life, residences on the old bridge were prized for the healthiness of the air, which given that the Thames already doubled as London's main sewer, doesn't say much for living conditions elsewhere. But during the height of the plague in 1665, when whole areas of London were ravaged, only two cases were recorded among inhabitants of the bridge.

Nevertheless, within eighty years of its completion 'the structure', according to the Victorian antiquarian Charles Welch, 'was so decayed that men were afraid to pass over it' and 'the history of the bridge', in his opinion, was to become 'a narrative of repairs'. It was also to become a narrative of England, with few major events passing it by – from the triumphant return of the Black Prince after the Battle of Poitiers and the Peasants' Revolt to the exhibition of William Wallace's and Thomas More's heads on the drawbridge and the Great Fire of London.

And in a sense, how could these events avoid London Bridge? Until 1729, it remained the sole fixed crossing over the Thames until Kingston.

And squatting on the river like a dragon jealously guarding its lair, spiky-backed with its houses, shops and severed heads on poles, the bridge nurtured an ecosystem that depended on its continuing dominance.*

Chief among those with a vested interest in the bridge's status quo were the river's watermen and lightermen. Every bit as vital, if equally intransigent, as their contemporary heirs, the black cabbies, these men were to view any suggestion of additional bridges, or improvements to the existing structure,

---

* The houses and shops would not be removed until the 1750s, the heads somewhat earlier in 1678, with William Sayley, a goldsmith executed for treason, supplying the last head to be exhibited on the bridge. One of the most outlandish things ever to grace Old London Bridge, however, was Nonsuch House (i.e. No Other Such House). A timber framed building with brilliantly ornate painted woodwork, carved gables, ostentatious cupolas and adorned with two sundials, it was erected in 1579. Nonsuch House had been built in Holland, and, in an eerie premonition of the fate of the later London Bridge, the whole building was shipped over, section by section, and then painstakingly reassembled on the southern end of the bridge.

as an affront to their profession. That profession was, to be fair, an extremely perilous one, consequently requiring by law a seven-year apprenticeship, and passing under – or 'shooting' – the bridge was by far the most dangerous part of it. On average, fifty of their number died each year in the churn of its arches or between its gouty piers – a mortality rate that naturally enough carried with it an attendant death toll of passengers. As a popular proverb catalogued by the naturalist Nicholas Ray in 1670 maintained, 'London Bridge was made for wise men to go over and fools to go under.' Cardinal Wolsey and Samuel Johnson, neither dullards, are both recorded studiously disembarking near the Vintry and hoofing it along the north bank to Billingsgate to avoid the bridge on river journeys out to Greenwich.

Like 1950s' fairground attendants risking life and limb on spinning waltzer rides, all Brylcreemed hair and exaggerated bravado, the watermen took a certain pride in this ever-present danger. Such hazards conferred status on the job. The ability to negotiate the Thames in any weather and tide, much more of a necessity when the only alternative to a boat was a single, crowded bridge, required knowledge and stamina, for which they were paid accordingly. As the conveyors of people, goods and messages they were trusted confidants, intimately aware of the comings and goings of the city. Capillaries that night and day kept the circulation of traffic flowing, they had been the lifeblood of the metropolis for centuries. Those who could not afford their fares were left, much as the dead on the banks of the Styx, to wander along the shore in misery. Their hold over the capital was formidable and, as assiduous lobbyists, they enjoyed considerable political influence. In the opening decades of the seventeenth century, when hackney carriages, a Continental import that looked like tempting people away from the river to the roads, first appeared, the Watermen's Company succeeded in excluding them from coming within two miles of the Thames. It is a measure of their clout – and their pigheadedness – that they ensured this ruling lasted for over thirty years.

When it came to protectionism, though, the watermen were more than matched by the City of London Corporation – the elected body that since medieval times, and as much by precedent as statute, has governed the City of London as a quasi-independent financial political fiefdom. Its power is such that it was the only local government body in the land to avoid reform in the 1830s – and today still possesses its own police force quite separate from the Met.

The Corporation took an especially dim view of anything that threatened to divert trade away from its environs. And London Bridge, as it stood, funnelled all those who entered London from the Surrey side into the Corporation's administrative and commercial clutches. This situation was a valuable enough asset in 1664 that the Corporation offered Charles II a £100,000 interest-free loan on the (tacit) understanding that he'd veto a scheme from the Privy Council to build a new bridge linking Lambeth and Westminster – the ecclesiastical and political quarters of the capital. The king took the money. The bishops at Lambeth, who could feasibly have benefitted most from a swifter route to and from Whitehall, had financial incentives of their own for discounting the plan. They held the rights to the Lambeth horse ferry and coined a healthy profit on its rent. With architectural energies soon diverted into rebuilding the City in the wake of the Great Fire, it was sixty years before this idea was formally resurrected again. Opposition then, however, proved just as fierce and in 1722 a bill for a bridge at Westminster was successfully defeated by a petition to Parliament supported by the Company of Watermen, the West Country Bargemen, the Borough of Southwark, the City and the residents of London Bridge itself.

Nevertheless, London's axis, a central east–west line, and hugger-mugger to the river, shifted decisively after the Great Fire of 1666. Where Piccadilly once marked the extreme western fringe of the capital, elegant new buildings were created north of it at Mayfair. If Oxford Street remained a 'deep hollow road full of sloughs' and 'the lurking place of cut-throats', the open fields between it and Hyde Park were fast being swallowed up by the brickwork and stucco of New Bond Street and Hanover Square. One rather excitable correspondent to *Applebee's Journal* described visiting these developments for the first time in 1725 and being confronted by 'an amazing scene of new foundations not of houses only . . . but . . . of new cities, new towns, new squares and fine buildings, the like of which no city, no town, no place in the world' could show. The scale of the work was so impressive that the writer found it impossible to judge when they would 'make an end, or stop building'.

Faced with such uninhibited expansion north and west, the compact burrow of the old city, despite extensive rebuilding, began to cut an embarrassingly mean shape – and one increasingly at odds with the nation's sense of itself as a growing mercantile power. The early Georgian Londoner with a single Thames span could only glance enviously across the channel to the Continent, to Paris, say, where the Seine was already criss-crossed by several bridges. Patriotism, as much as progress, was at stake.

A rubicon was crossed, more literally than metaphorically, in 1729 when a bridge was finally erected at Fulham, bringing London Bridge's isolation to an end. This had originally been suggested in 1671 by John Dwight, the owner of a local pottery. But the City and the ferrymen had little trouble in seeing off the proposal back then. Denouncing it as a wild and silly scheme, they argued it would block the river, cause flooding, and cause the destruction of the City itself by luring commerce west. Giving full expression to this apocalyptic theme, Sir William Thompson, a prominent London politician and one-time governor of the East India Company, warned Parliament that 'when the walls of London shall no longer be visible and Ludgate is demolished, England itself shall be as nothing'.

Some fifty years on, however, the de facto prime minister Sir Robert Walpole, riding back to the Commons from an audience with George I in Kingston, was infuriated to be left stranded on the bank at Putney. The ferrymen snubbed him, choosing to forgo the fare to carry on drinking at the Swan Inn on the Fulham side instead. Presumably Walpole took the long way back to Westminster, for once there he wasted no time in petitioning for a toll bridge to be built on the site of his humiliation. An Act of Parliament authorising its construction was passed in 1726 and Walpole himself invested £1,000 in the venture.

Five years later, and clearly emboldened by the Fulham example, a group calling themselves 'a Society of Gentlemen' and led by Lord Henry Herbert, 9th Earl of Pembroke, one of a number of aristocratic tastemakers who were proselytisers for Palladian architecture in Hanoverian Britain, formed to promote the new bridge at Westminster.

It was eventually erected in 1750. Designed in stone by the Swiss engineer Charles Labelye, it was a rather fetching, if ultimately insubstantial (it lasted just seventy years), example of the advanced neoclassical. Painted some twenty times by Canaletto and the subject of a poem by Wordsworth, it soon made London Bridge appear distinctly old hat by comparison. Accordingly in 1756, the City Surveyor, George Dance the Elder, embarked on a programme of works to modernise London Bridge. Most significantly this involved widening its clogged roadway from twelve feet to forty-five feet by shearing the bridge of its jagged mane of shops and houses. By the end of 1762, Old London Bridge was as bald as a plucked chicken, and, rather like Samson after his run-in with Delilah, was judged to cut a noticeably feebler figure about the place for it. And with the arrival of yet another Thames crossing – Blackfriars Bridge by Robert Mylne a mere seven years later – its status in the cityscape diminished still further. But a major impetus for its eventual replacement, amusingly given later events, was to come from further afield: America – and from one of the great champions of revolution and independence.

CHAPTER 2

I Am Iron, Man

Tucked away in an underwhelming square that forms the entrance to an anonymous complex of buildings huddled beside the Angel Tube station, Islington, there is a memorial to Thomas Paine. The political radical, opponent of aristocratic tyranny and author of *Rights of Man* appears in profile on a queasy green-bronze obelisk adorned with stars and keys and dotted with quotes from his works. 'LAY THEN THE AXE TO THE ROOT AND TEACH GOVERNMENTS HUMANITY' runs one, twinned with an embossed representation of a shrub decapitating itself with an axe. Paine himself looks jowly, with a weak chin, but a strong nose and a thick head of tangled hair that is swept back in a fashion that suggests fingers, no doubt ink-stained and pretty grubby, were often pulled through it during intense periods of concentration or argument. As a failed tobacconist with an aversion to washing and a prodigious thirst for alcohol, and the man who helped establish the Bank of Philadelphia – America's first bank – it's fitting that his memorial's most constant companions are street drinkers and smokers from the nearby offices of the Royal Bank of Scotland.

This monument, the only one dedicated to Paine in the capital, commemorates his residence here in around 1790, when he is supposed to have written parts of his most famous work while staying at the Red Lion inn on what is now St John Street. *Rights of Man* was famously written as a response – a rebuttal – to the Tory parliamentarian and philosopher Edmund Burke's denunciations of the French Revolution. Less well known, perhaps, is that Burke and Paine had been friends. And shortly before their spat, the pair had spent several companionable weeks together travelling around England visiting foundries and exploring potential sites for a new type of iron bridge that Paine himself had designed back in Pennsylvania after retiring from the hurly-burly of American political life in 1783.

Bridge building might seem far removed from political revolutions and pamphleteering, but this foray into civil engineering was really just a further instantiation of Paine's Enlightenment principles. He had no formal mechanical training. Born in Thetford in Norfolk in 1737 as Thomas Pain – the 'e' came and went, but in keeping with countless transatlantic reinventions, became a permanent fixture after his arrival in America in 1774 – he was the son of a Quaker staymaker. But he was also a classic autodidact and he impressed Benjamin Franklin (no slouch in the field) with the breadth of his reading in science and mathematics when they first met in London in the late 1750s. And once the war for American Independence was won, Paine's stated ambition was to spend the rest of his days toiling in what he called 'the quiet field of science'. And it was America, or more accurately Philadelphia where he had first settled in the States, that was to nudge him in the direction of civil engineering.

Founded by the Quaker William Penn, 'the city of brotherly love' (then also known as 'the Athens of America' because of its reputation as a centre of learning) sits upon the banks of the Schuylkill River. Each spring Paine had observed that after the frozen winter months, the melting river became an astonishing torrent of ice floes that no conventional bridge, with its numerous piers and arches of wood and stone, would ever be able to withstand for long. In France some years earlier, however, he had come across schemes proposed by a Monsieur de Montpetit to build single iron-arched bridges. Believing something similar might be applicable for

Philadelphia, by 1786 he had drawn up plans for a lightweight bridge of a single 400-foot span of iron for the Schuylkill that would leave 'the whole passage of the river clear of the encumbrance of piers'. Describing its inspiration in a letter to Sir George Staunton, the Irish-born diplomat, botanist and member of the Royal Society in London, Paine was moved to evoke the turmoil of the revolution and the geography and psyche of his newly independent nation:

> The natural mightiness of America expands the mind, and it partakes of the greatness it contemplates. Even the war, with all its evils, had some advantages. It energized invention and lessened the catalogue of impossibilities. At the conclusion of it every man returned to his home to repair the ravages it had occasioned, and to think of war no more. As one amongst thousands who had borne a share in that memorable revolution, I returned with them to the re-enjoyment of quiet life, and, that I might not be idle, undertook to construct a bridge of a single arch for this river.

If a model, exhibited at the State House in Boston in December 1786, impressed everyone with its ingenuity, no one in America seemed willing to invest more than a nominal stake in such an untested technological advance. With his fiftieth birthday approaching, Paine decided to act on some advice from his friend Benjamin Franklin and seek out other sponsors in Europe, sailing for France in 1787. But with Louis XVI's France on the brink of fiscal collapse, he again found backers thin on the ground and so he travelled to London.

Having lodged another model of the bridge with the Royal Society in the hope of gaining their endorsement, in September 1788 he took out a patent – no. 1,667 – for 'A method of constructing of arches . . . on principles new and different to anything hitherto practised' and embarked on a tour of the country to find possible locations for his bridge – often with Edmund Burke in tow. That autumn Paine also visited Walkers of Rotherham, at that time one of the leading iron foundries in the country, and managed to convince them to build a prototype. Completed in April 1789, this bridge was comprised of a single iron archway of just ninety feet and was barely five feet in height. (To Paine's frustration, Walkers, lacking the space in their foundry to store it, had scrimped on the scale.) Nevertheless, it was shown to be capable of bearing a weight of six tons of pig iron. Paine was especially gratified to discover his bridge had become the talk of Rotherham. 'It is commended,' he wrote, quill pen no doubt gripped rather firmly in excitement, 'even by the Ladies who tho' they may not be acquainted with Mathematical principles, are certainly Judges of Taste.'

Buoyed by this response, Paine set his sights on London as the site for his bridge. Walkers were persuaded to construct a further prototype – a hundred-foot span to be built of five ribs of iron – which he then aimed to have erected over the River Thames. This plan, alas, was never to be realised. But his second prototype did make its debut in London. Unlikely as it may seem now, it was exhibited at the Yorkshire Stingo public house in Lisson Grove,

Paddington in May 1790. City public houses and coaching inns in this still pre-railway age, it must be borne in mind, remained major transport hubs and retained their overhanging galleries and spacious front courtyards, kept stables, and offered rooms to let. Arguably they were far closer to something like a modern airport, with its arrival hall and departure lounges, duty-free shops, food stalls, hotels and car parks, than the sticky-carpeted, fruit-machine-stuffed London boozers of more recent lore. Therefore, it can only be presumed that the Yorkshire Stingo itself, lying in Paddington, then an outlying village gradually being subsumed into the expanding metropolis, had some kind of hall or circus-style 'showground' as punters had to pay a shilling a go to marvel at Paine's miracle of the nascent Industrial Revolution.

Some forty years later George Shillibeer would launch his horse-drawn omnibus service from outside the same pub, an event that reconfigured at a stroke all previous ideas about navigating the capital for work or pleasure. And those who did come to gawp at Paine's bridge most likely met a proposition almost as discombobulating for its period. If the surviving drawings and notes leave the precise technical details of its construction a bit vague 200-odd years on – a lattice of iron ribs modelled after a spider's web is a recurring description – it appears to have surpassed any extant bridge with the intricacy of its construction. But what possibly could have lent it an added edge was that the design quite consciously looked forward to a day when bridge building could be largely a matter of assembly. Paine confidently (and correctly) predicted that relatively lightweight iron sections could be mass-produced and then 'sent to any part of the world to be erected'.

By the late eighteenth century, iron bridges were, of course, far from novelties in Europe. There is even some evidence to suggest that a seventy-foot iron arch was erected at Kirkgate in Yorkshire as early as 1770, and on New Year's Day 1781 Abraham Darby III's hundred-foot span over the Severn Gorge near Coalbrookdale in Shropshire had been unveiled. Darby's 'Iron Bridge' – '*The* Iron Bridge' – had been immediately greeted as a major spectacle. Its image, conveyed via drawings and etchings commissioned by its proprietors from Michael Angelo Rooker, the Haymarket Theatre's scene-painter and a Royal Academician, and reproduced in cheap souvenir prints, quickly became one of the most recognisable of the age.

Intruding on the landscape in ways that some found quite terrifying, iron bridges were soon to change the look of the world along with presenting fresh vantage points to *look at* the world. Genuinely awe-inspiring to Romantic artists such as Constable and Turner, they were unlike anything seen before. Nevertheless, many of the earliest iron bridges, Darby's included, were in reality structurally little different from their wooden and stone forebears – despite the originality of their materials. Which is why Paine's entry into the field at this point remains so fascinating. Not only did his design differ from those that had gone before, but his engagement with the mechanical sciences also lent an added soupçon of heroism to them. As a radical philosopher-engineer, he thus became something of a role model to the likes of Thomas

Telford, the first president of the Institution of Civil Engineers, and through them his bridge was to exert a subtle if pervasive influence on several future structures, not least the new London Bridge.

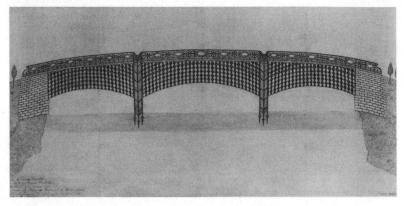

Political events across the Channel were to drag Paine away from what he called the 'portable manufacture' of bridges. Though he would not have known it, by 1791 he had finished with bridges for good. By the following year the author of *Rights of Man* was in Paris. There he sat as a member of the French Convention until falling out with Robespierre over Louis XVI's execution and only narrowly escaped the guillotine himself. Eventually returning to America, severely weakened after two years in a Parisian gaol, he was greeted, not as a returning champion of democracy but as an embarrassing hangover of a less advanced, and less godly, republic. A John the Baptist who hadn't had the decency to get himself beheaded, he was maligned as an atheistic rabble-rouser, a man still needlessly munching on locusts and honey when there were twelve baskets of fish and loaves for the snacking. Dying in hooch-sodden near-penury in a flophouse in Greenwich Village, New York, in 1809, he was later defamed in the American press as 'a drunken coward' who had died 'a drunken, cowardly and beastly death'. Hardly a generous epitaph for a man who, if not shy of a brandy and perhaps more cranky uncle than Founding Father, had, nevertheless, stoked the fires of the Revolution.

As for his prototype iron bridge, after its run at the Yorkshire Stingo, it was broken up for scrap and shipped back to Walkers of Rotherham. However, such was its fame that small pieces of it are known to have been spirited away from their yard by souvenir hunters, while the appearance of a remarkably similar-looking iron bridge over the Wear in Sunderland, also cast by Walkers, led many to suspect that the Yorkshire firm had taken that county's famed thriftiness to new lengths. Indeed for a century or more it was widely rumoured that the Wearmouth Bridge, affectionately referred to as 'the stupendous iron arch', was basically Paine's bridge reassembled, or large chunks of it anyway. That Walkers might perhaps have recycled some elements of its raw materials can't be dismissed entirely; any old iron would, to paraphrase the song, do. But most experts today argue that it is extremely unlikely, if not actually impossible, that any of Paine's ironmongery, the latticed 'spider' ribs for example, found its way up to Sunderland. For one thing, the Wearmouth was a much larger and simpler bridge. It was, in fact, the largest single-span bridge in the world when it was completed in 1796. Boasting a lone span of 236 feet, its iron arch, supported on stone piers at either side, stood at nearly a hundred feet in height. What is in little doubt, though, is that Paine's prototype inspired its construction.* But since Paine's efforts failed to get beyond a London pub (telling perhaps), it was this Mackem whippersnapper, derived from his basic idea, that was to lap up all the acclaim – and, gallingly, among the very movers and shakers the writer had wanted to court in London. Still, as a fully functioning iron bridge, and one that with a patch or three here and there lasted until 1929, the Wearmouth was a step forward for domestic industrial architecture.

The Wearmouth Bridge was the brainchild of Rowland Burdon, a wealthy local landowner, merchant banker, MP for County Durham, mayor of Stockton and leading Freemason who almost single-handedly financed the project. Burdon spent some years soliciting a suitable design and went through a number of different architects – including John Nash of Regent Street fame, who was hired and then fired after submitting a scheme for a masonry arch deemed 'unfeasible'.† In the end, Burdon was credited with coming up with the plan for an iron bridge himself. How much of a hand Burdon actually had in the nuts and bolts of this plan is debatable.

---

* Though the writer's span with its latticework was, if anything, a more sophisticated affair than the Wearmouth, which mimicked techniques ordinarily deployed on stone bridges. In engineering terms, his prototype was practically the *Discovery One* spaceship to the Wear's ape-tossed animal bone.

† This dismissal was to needle the architect for decades to come. In 1811, during a party at his lavish Isle of Wight estate, Nash told the assembled guests that the finished Wearmouth was entirely his work and complained that the design had been stolen from him.

Nearly all of the technical detail (admittedly not unusually for this period and far beyond it) was provided by his engineer Thomas Wilson, aided by Joshua Walker – the head of the Rotherham iron foundry behind both of Paine's prototypes.

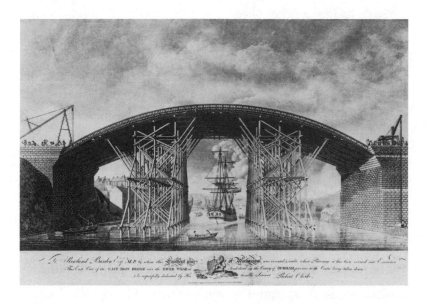

Down in London, news of the Wearmouth Bridge's formidable span excited admiration, if not outright jealousy. That jobbing sailing ships, their masts fully rigged and holds teeming with coal, were able to pass beneath its high metal canopy was widely commented upon in the City.

Casting his eye over the Thames and at the decaying stone piers of Old London Bridge, Sir Frederick Morton Eden couldn't help blushing positively crimson in shame when he thought about the Wearmouth. The son of the last Royal Governor of Maryland in America, and the author of a groundbreaking three-volume study of the living conditions of the poor, Eden saw in Sunderland's arch a solution to a specific set of problems then afflicting the capital's riverfront.

Visiting London in 1790, the Welsh antiquarian Thomas Pennant had found the Thames east of London Bridge so dense with ships that it 'presented a double forest of masts'. Agreeably sylvan as this image is, Pennant's description captures the degree to which the river was fast becoming impossibly congested. While global trade in the second half of the eighteenth century rocketed in sync with Britain's reach as a coming imperial power, facilities at the Port of London were not keeping pace with these developments. Between 1700 and 1790, the import and export trade it handled rose from £10,263,325 to £22,992,004 – an increase of 124 per cent. Yet the offloading of ocean-borne goods remained a distressingly Herculean labour. There were only a handful of private docks in operation – among them Mr Perry's dock at Blackwall, Execution Dock at Wapping and St Saviour's at Southwark. The majority of traffic used the moorings on the Thames, which stretched in an almost unbroken line downstream from London Bridge to Limehouse on the north bank and Deptford on the south. And once moored all vessels had to go through the arduous and, since pilfering was rife, costly business of waiting to decant their cargoes into open barges or small boats called lighters which ferried them to various designated quays and riverside warehouses for unloading. It was sometimes claimed that it cost more to get a cargo of skins across the Thames from

Wapping than it did to get them over the Atlantic from Hudson Bay.

With the gradual entwining of imperial and commercial concerns in India and the Caribbean, these arrangements became more obviously untenable. Calls to improve the port, led by demands in Parliament for the construction of efficient wet docks at Wapping and the Isle of Dogs where the comings and goings of tea, wine, brandy, rice, tobacco and spices and so on could be monitored (where necessary) by excise men, grew shrill as conflict with France depleted the Treasury coffers and the century began tapering to its end.

Adding a fresh note to this chorus, and with the Wearmouth as his template, in 1798 – the same year that a Marine Police Force was established to guard the Pool of London – Eden proposed replacing the Old London Bridge of fang-like cutwaters with a taller iron crossing of five wide arches. The new bridge would be capacious enough to allow taller and broader 200-ton ships to sail under it. If these larger seafaring vessels were able to reach beyond the bridge, he argued, then there was scope for new port facilities along the Thames as far as Blackfriars. Coupled with sketches of the warehouses and two small docks he suggested could be built, Eden's plans were greeted enthusiastically by architects and politicians alike.

In comparison with Sunderland, however, where the banks stood far above the Wear, giving the bridge a kind of leg-up over the water, an obstacle for anyone attempting something even vaguely similar at London Bridge was the relatively low-lying land on either side of the river. To build a bridge with sufficient height for ships but with approaches and a roadway that were level enough for people on foot and horse-driven vehicles to use remained a technical challenge – and one that some of the liveliest minds in engineering felt Eden hadn't adequately addressed. Responding in the spirit of gentlemanly, if mildly admonishing and fervid competition that accompanied nearly every civic speculation in this era, Ralph Dodd was the first to counter with a design of his own.

Dodd, who in that same year also unveiled the scheme for a tunnel under the Thames from Tilbury to Gravesend which was to end in ignominious failure, was never short of ideas. Luck, sadly, was another matter. Portraits depict him with a noticeably triangular head dripping to an icicle chin set off by a tiny, pursed mouth. Much like a bag of chips doused in vinegar, sourness appears to be oozing through the bottom of his face. Though inadequate dental hygiene probably had as much to do with that physiognomy as any career disappointments. A native of Tyneside thwarted in his attempts to equip Sunderland with docks, Dodd was a one-time budding artist who, despite advancing the course of inland navigation in this country and sharing a patent for an embryonic steam locomotive with George Stephenson, died in poverty with many of his boldest dreams – a canal snaking from Rotherhithe to Southampton via Epsom, to name but one – unrealised.

Working from Eden's basic conceit, Dodd furnished projective drawings of an iron bridge dominated by a central 300-foot span, looming some hundred feet over the Thames. When they were exhibited the following year at the Royal Academy of Arts, where he had studied painting, Dodd claimed that rigged hulks of up to 600 tons would be able to negotiate his bridge as easily as any barge.

While Dodd was wooing the academy with his drawings, James Douglass, an ambitious young Scottish engineer with three patents to his name, entered the fray, publishing a pamphlet outlining his proposal for an asymmetrical five-arch iron bridge that adhered, numerically at least, much more keenly to Eden's original scheme. With each of these bridge designs offering the irresistible option of extending the capacity of the Port of London, a parliamentary select committee was formed in May 1799 to consider the whole question of redeveloping its provisions.

In the coming months, this committee would give its approval to bills on the construction of the West India Docks at the Isle of Dogs and the London Docks at Wapping under the direction of the prominent engineers William Jessop and John Rennie respectively, and order a further study to be prepared on the bridge and shipping in London. Published on 11 July 1799, this 'Second Report upon the Improvement of the Port of London' now left few in any doubt about Old London Bridge's fate.

The nineteenth century, then, would begin with Parliament ordering the committee to solicit further designs for a brand new London Bridge. And in April 1800, just thirteen years after Paine had returned to England desperate to import fresh thinking from America in the form of a New World bridge, they launched a competition to find a successor worthy of replacing de Colechurch's historic crossing.

CHAPTER 3

The Bridges London Never Had

The opportunity to equip London with a new – *its* new – bridge was a challenge that few of the leading figures in engineering wished to miss. The select committee receiving an assortment of notable submissions was left with half a dozen compellingly different options to pursue. That it succeeded in pursuing none of them can be chalked up as another of London's great spurned opportunities – something, if you are feeling grandiloquent, on a par with Wren's failed Great Fire rebuilding plans, or at least as disappointing as the abrupt curtailing to Camberwell of the Grand Union Canal.

One of those who applied themselves to the problem of the new bridge for the Thames was Thomas Wilson, the engineer on the Wearmouth Bridge. His offering to London was a three-span iron bridge fixed on masonry piers and abutments. Though attractive in form and structurally quite similar to the Sunderland crossing, modern engineers note severe technical flaws in the design – the abutments appear far too slender to have ever adequately supported the span and there is not enough cross-bracing, apparently, between the ribs. Another cast-iron bridge, propped up, on this occasion, by rather sturdier-looking piers to be fashioned of granite, came in the form of a model submitted by Samuel Wyatt, architect (with

John Rennie) of the Albion Flour Mills at Southwark, one of London's earliest factories.

Ralph Dodd, in a bravura rethink of his earlier proposal, produced drawings for two monumental stone crossings: one with six arches and a central span of 300 feet in width, and another with five arches and a middle arch of 160 feet. Both came with adjacent schemes for quayside warehouses and docks.

A further stone structure of five arches was put forward by Robert Mylne, the Scottish engineer–architect behind Blackfriars Bridge thirty years earlier and shortly tasked with helping organise Nelson's funeral. Aware of this historical titbit, it becomes hard not to project a slightly morbid aspect on to Mylne's scheme for London Bridge. Under his plan a much expanded approach road on the northern bank was to lead on to a grand new piazza developed around the Monument – the City's lofty tribute to the Great Fire and its (admittedly only five or six) incinerated victims.

Resurrecting the idea outlined in his earlier pamphlet, James Douglass, this time joined by fellow Scot Thomas Telford, furnished a design for an asymmetric iron bridge. The largest arch here was closest to the higher north bank with the expressed aim of producing a bridge whose gradient, overall, was marginally easier going. Despite a nascent Gothic revival, the committee – gentlemen schooled in the pleasing order of neoclassicism – were not likely to sanction replacing an edifice hailing from the Plantagenet era with a newfangled one as crook-backed as Richard III. Indeed, Douglass' bridge was judged to be 'so disagreeable in appearance' that they didn't even have the drawings of it engraved for wider consideration. Douglass and Telford, possibly mindful of this reaction, supplied further illustrations for less lopsided three- and five-arch bridges and a bolder plan for a single iron bridge spanning 600 feet. These were deemed more acceptable. In a move that suggests favour-currying patriotic overkill – or since it emanated from two Scots less than a century after the Union, overcompensation – the latter design was supposedly to be adorned with statues celebrating England's naval victories.*

But then Telford, perhaps more than Douglass, who soon receded from view in any case, needed to prove his allegiance. The son of a shepherd who died before his son was four months old, Telford was born in the rural parish of Westerkirk in Eskdale, Scotland, in 1757. And his trajectory from abject peat-bog poverty to burial in Westminster Abbey with all the frills reads like an especially heavy-handed three-decker novel. Lessons about dignity in the face of adversity, the value of hard work and the socially elevating power of literature and education are there in spades, while its cast list – heavy on formidable widows, nurturing blind village schoolteachers, cruel master masons, encouraging wealthy spinsters and decent poetry-loving aristocratic patrons – sails close to parody when eyed today. Only a romantic interest appears missing – and Telford, who died a bachelor, never seems to have shown much inclination in that department. This is, of course, to devalue the extraordinary and unique obstacles a man apprenticed

---

* Think how much further they would have got if they'd suggested covering it with replicas of traitors' heads – commencing with William Wallace, say . . .

to a thuggish stonecutter at fifteen overcame to become the pre-eminent civil engineer of his age. One not inconsiderable hurdle was the suggestion, in polite society at least, that Telford was politically suspect.

His great hero was Thomas Paine, whom he admired as a thinker and whose cast-iron span provided an impetus to his own experiments with the same element for large bridges and viaducts. Telford was to build his first iron bridge in 1796 at Buildwas in Shropshire – where he was the County Surveyor of Public Works, an appointment he held for life from 1787. His connections to that region were formally put on the map when the Dawley New Town Development Corporation opted to name their new town 'Telford' in his honour in 1968. But Telford originally came to Shropshire at the behest of his longstanding patron (and yet another Scot), Sir William Pulteney, MP for Shrewsbury, to restore Shrewsbury Castle.

It was an event which sorely tested the relationship between Pulteney and Telford that led to the latter's longstanding reputation as a man of questionable political leaning. In around 1793 Telford, now resident in Shrewsbury and enjoying Pulteney's munificence, had sent a copy of Paine's *Rights of Man* to Andrew Little, his old blind teacher in Langholm, under Pulteney's postage frank. Since Little relied on others to read new books to him, this volume, or at worst a garbled precis of its contents, quickly circulated around the Esk Valley. The book was then blamed for inciting a mini riot. A group calling themselves 'the Langholm

Patriots' and seemingly overwhelmed by the force of Paine's arguments, and no less empathetic to his bibulous tendencies, drank a series of 'revolutionary toasts at the Cross'. Rounded up for causing a breach of the peace, some of them were confined to the county gaol for six weeks. While the incident didn't affect their relationship in the long term, Telford was given a severe dressing-down by his incensed and conservative patron, and a reputation as a political radical continued to dog him when he established a base in London in 1800.

That year, he took up residence at the Salopian Coffee House in Charing Cross and remained there until 1821. The Salopian was, for Telford, a home, a business headquarters and a salon rolled into one. A gregarious soul, he saw visitors at all hours, and welcomed any opportunity to discourse at length on any engineering problem.

Legend has it that he was considered such a fixture his presence was included in the goodwill of the business. When he eventually came to give notice, the landlord, who had only recently taken possession of the establishment, was reputedly horrified. 'What! Leave the house!' he exclaimed. 'Why, sir, I have just paid £750 for you.' The ratebooks, which don't show any change of ownership at that point, alas make this exchange, if no less revealing as fiction, distinctly unlikely.

At the time of the London Bridge contest, though, Telford remained a fresh addition to the city's luminaries. But perhaps among the most intriguing, and fiercest, challenge he and Douglass

faced for the prize came from an establishment insider: George
Dance the Younger, the Architect and Surveyor to the Corporation
of London.

A founding member of the Royal Academy and its professor
of architecture for seven years, as a young man Dance had travelled extensively in Italy and was profoundly influenced by the
classical antiquities and buildings he saw there. Training under
his father, who had overseen the removal of the houses on Old
London Bridge and whose office as surveyor he inherited, Dance
played a definitive role in loosening the City out of its medieval
shackles. Credited with introducing the circus and the crescent
into London street-planning, he was responsible for equipping the
south bank below Blackfriars Bridge, then a dank expanse of
stinking marshland leavened by the odd glass-worker's cottage,
with a respiratory system of new roads that converged at an obelisk
at St George's Circus.

And an obelisk would prove just one notable feature of Dance's
London Bridge scheme. Positioned on a grand piazza at the south
side of his new bridge, it was intended to mirror the Monument.
Much like Mylne's plan, this too was to become the focal point of
another new square on the north bank. There, in a sense, all other
similarities between his design and any of the other contenders
ended. Where his rivals, following the committee's brief, dealt with
the question of headroom for ships by proffering bridges of impressive height, Dance came up with something entirely different. What
makes his design especially fascinating is that it contains the seeds

of an idea that would reach fruition in Tower Bridge nearly a century later.

Dance's London Bridge was to be composed of two separate stone bridges of six arches set side by side. Each had a drawbridge in its centre to allow ships to pass, and was flanked by two towers housing the machinery to control the bascules, i.e. the lifty-up bits. All the key elements of Tower Bridge are there, in effect; if laid out horizontally in series rather than stacked vertically. As such it comes somewhere near the Earl of Sandwich's early efforts with 'two slices of turkey with a slice of bread in the middle' in the Woody Allen parody *Yes, But Can the Steam Engine Do This?* Nevertheless, Dance's scheme, with its twin crossings, towers, drawbridges, twin piazzas, banks of Venetian-style steps descending to the river and obelisk, had originality, symmetry and grandeur on its side. But originality, symmetry and grandeur are never cheap. And Dance's price for sweeping aside centuries of inept bankside making-do-and-mend was an eye-watering £1.25 million.

Though perhaps more naturally predisposed to favour the splendour of Dance's plan, if less easy with the cost, the committee kept returning to Telford's and Douglass' span. Its image, a lace of ironwork, taunted them with its racy modernity. It offered the possibility of a London where frigates could go all the way up the Thames, and cruising for trade was easier. This bridge would be a visual spectacle, dominating the landscape, but also a gallery, allowing the blooming metropolis itself to be contemplated as an object of desire and wonder.

The thorniest issue continued, however, to be the untested nature of this structure's technology. If the survival of Abraham Darby III's Iron Bridge in the disastrous Severn River floods of 1795 – a torrent that swept every other bridge in the region away – helped turn iron into a matter of engineering faith for Telford himself, and if Burdon had demonstrated the strength of the Wearmouth Bridge by having 1,000 militiamen from the Royal Tay Fencibles march across it, there were many counter-examples of these new metal crossings collapsing under quite pitiful weights. An early outing in iron by John Nash at Dodington, for one, collapsed when a single small boy tramped across it in the winter of 1795. The child in question escaped unharmed, but fearing the adverse publicity, the iron makers at Coalbrookdale issued notices in the Midlands press stating categorically that Nash's bridge had not been cast in their foundry.

To this day, there remain some doubts about exactly how practical Telford's London Bridge with its reach of 600 feet would have been. Apart from its length, which admittedly was a substantial and possibly risky imaginative leap, its engineering, if tipping a hat to the advances of Paine and the Wearmouth, was reasonably perfunctory. Could such a structure have ever really coped with thousands upon thousands of people, and their dogs, cattle, sheep, geese, horses, coaches and wagons traipsing back and forth across it, in and out of the capital, each and every day?

A committee was commissioned to conduct an extensive study into its feasibility, and called in the likes of steam-engine pioneer James Watt, the iron founder John Wilkinson, Nevil Maskelyne, the Astronomer Royal, and the civil engineer John Rennie to assess the design. The canal builder William Reynolds expressed some concern that dangers could arise if 'vibrations from 9-ton wagons became isochronous with the vibrations of the bridge' – a prognosis of the same 'wobbly bridge' problem that duly afflicted Foster + Partners' 'blade of light' Millennium Bridge in 2000. But the consensus was that Telford's bridge could, and indeed should, be built.

After taking in additional findings from a study of the Thames by William Jessop, the designer of the West India Docks, the committee therefore recommended that London Bridge should be replaced by an iron bridge, sixty-five feet above high water, and that the river should be embanked, and warehouses built on the embankments from the bridge to Blackfriars. But events had over-taken it. In the year since Parliament first recommended the bridge, the world had changed. Now, with Napoleon menacing Austria and riots breaking out on the streets of London over the rising cost of bread, Parliament evidently believed it had other priorities, and so asked for the report to be 'laid on the Table'.

Its papers would grow mottled and brown to the colour of urn-stewed tea before anything further was done.

CHAPTER 4

Take Rennie

On the evening of 27 December 1813, an icy fog swirled in over London. Described as 'a darkness that might be felt', its immense and oppressive gloom was to reach as far as the South Downs seventy miles away and did not disperse for seven full days. In that time, few left their homes. The city slumped into an uneasy enforced silence: just the cries of nightwatchmen, the clatter of an odd carriage cautiously feeling its way through the miasma, the dull insistent thud of forefingers prodding at the pages of prayer books and Bibles, as litanies were whispered and verses inspected for prophetic meaning ('He sent darkness, and it was dark', Psalms, 105:28). The fog lifted by 3 January but temperatures now dropped and heavy snow fell for two days.

Down by the river, the surface of the Thames glistened with chunks of floating ice. Splintering and creaking as the tide carried them towards London Bridge, they knotted together to form great bergs that clustered in the weaker midstream and around the bridge. With a loud bang and a rush of foam, these were sucked with terrifying force through the narrow arches as the river valiantly attempted to retain its normal flow. Growing ever more soporific as the cold spell continued, the river finally succumbed to complete immobility.

Heading out on the morning of 1 February, Londoners found that the watermen had placed signs at the ends of all river-bound city streets, informing them that the Thames, now several feet thick with ice in places, was safe to walk on. The watermen were not acting out of civic duty, they extracted entrance fees from those who made their way to the fast-assembling 'frost fair'.

Nicknamed 'the City Road', the frozen surface of the river from Blackfriars Bridge to the Three Crane Stairs near Cheapside was transformed into a bustling promenade and lined with booths decorated with colourful flags and streamers, selling gin, grog, tea, coffee and gingerbread. Games of skittles and dances were held. 'Eight or ten' printing presses set up shop, producing broadsides commemorating 'the Great Frost' on the ice. These were hawked as souvenirs to the passing crowds. Indicating the somewhat simpler pleasures of the era, one of the biggest draws was a mutton roasting stall, with punters forking out sixpence each merely to watch the spectacle of a small sheep browning over a coal fire in an hefty iron pan. The meat, when done, was then sold as 'Lapland Mutton' for a shilling a slice.

Not all the river was quite this sturdy, however. A plumber named Davit, having, in the words of one contemporary observer, 'imprudently ventured to cross with some lead in his hands' at a point near Blackfriars, sank between two masses of ice and was drowned.

On the evening of the fourth day of the fair, it rained, and a crack appeared in the ice and the whole surface rapidly began to

FROSTIANA:

OR

A HISTORY OF

THE RIVER THAMES,

In a Frozen State;

WITH AN ACCOUNT OF

THE LATE SEVERE FROST;

AND THE WONDERFUL EFFECTS

OF

Frost, Snow, Ice, and Cold,

IN ENGLAND,

AND IN DIFFERENT PARTS OF THE WORLD;

INTERSPERSED

WITH VARIOUS AMUSING ANECDOTES.

TO WHICH IS ADDED,

THE ART OF SKATING.

A *dreadful winter* came; *each day* severe,
Misty when mild, and *icy-cold* when clear.
CRABBE.

London:

Printed and published on the ICE on the River *Thames,*
February 5, 1814, by G. DAVIS.

Sold also by Sherwood, Neely, and Jones, Paternoster Row.

shift and dissolve, carrying off several hastily abandoned booths and resulting in at least two further fatalities. By the next day, the river, swelled by the melting ice, thrashed about like a fairy-tale giant awoken from a deep sleep. Dotted with fragments of ice, the wreckage of lighters seized from their moorings and detritus from the fair, it thundered wildly into London Bridge, pummelling its abutments and arches.

The damage it wreaked on the bridge that year would have the long-term consequence of ensuring that city folk were never to frolic on its glacial strata again.

In a similar frost in 1282, ice had reputedly succeeded in heaving away four of the bridge's original nineteen arches. The stone bridge was a relative newcomer to the Thames then, and in the centuries of winters to follow it would grow frostbitten from a succession of comparable bouts with the river. The Great Frost of 1814 would, in a sense, turn out to be a pyrrhic victory for Old Father Thames, at least in its frostiest incarnation.

Once the ice of the Great Frost had departed, the bridge was revealed to be in a worse state than ever before. A report delivered to the Corporation of London that November by Messrs (George) Dance, Chapman, Alexander and Montague advised removing four of the bridge's piers and converting its eight arches into four. This, it was argued, would allow the water to pass under the bridge more easily and stop the build-up of ice in the winter months.

But prevarication and inaction once again ruled, and two new bridges, Vauxhall and Waterloo, opened in 1816 and 1817 respectively, were standing over the Thames before this proposition was examined in detail again. Those young pretenders on the Thames almost embarrassed the government into action over London Bridge, their lithe iron and stone bodies only emphasising its pitiful decay. In any case, in 1821 Ralph Dodd was charged with having yet another poke about to monitor the state of the bridge and discovered a chasm nearly four feet deep in the starling on the north side of the central arch.

Such findings were to throw severe doubt on the prudence of spending anything like the £92,000 Dance and Co. had estimated their improvements would cost. What was the point of undertaking yet another round of expensive repairs if the bridge was getting close to irreparable, anyway?

Deeming any additional repairs uncertain, and wastefully expensive, a select committee of the Bridge House Estates recommended that the House of Commons should pass a bill authorising the construction of a new London Bridge. In due course, and just over twenty years since the last competition, a further call for new designs went out with sums of £250, £150 and £100 being offered for the three most promising entries. A panel comprising John Nash, John Soane and Robert Smirke, then all members of the royal household's Office of Works, and City architect William Montague was assembled to judge submissions. The engineer John Rennie, meanwhile, had been employed by the Corporation of London to conduct a thorough survey of the river and its tides – from

Teddington Lock to the west down to the new London Docks at Wapping in the east.

The panel, after considering some forty-eight submissions ranging from crackpot sketches knocked off by budding Christopher Wrens to formal costed plans from some of the finest architects in the land, awarded the main prize to Joseph Gwilt.

The Southwark-born son of the Surveyor of Buildings and Land for the county of Surrey, author of *A Treatise on the Equilibrium of Arches* and a fellow of the Society of Antiquaries of London, Gwilt was dubbed 'the sworn champion of Palladianism' by the *Civil Engineer and Architect's Journal* – which in the second decade of the nineteenth century was probably less of an unambiguous compliment than it once had been. His five-arch stone design for London Bridge nevertheless appears a model of the Italian style in England; symmetrical and discreetly Continental, the building equivalent of Pizza Express, say, with the 25p discretionary donation paid in full to the Venetian fund. That it should appeal to Nash, Soane and Smirke, architects with a fondness for the classics, is not much of a surprise. Gwilt was an architect after their own hearts: urbane, travelled, with a scholarly yet practical interest in art history, linguistics and mathematics. That the City's Court of Common Council would reject their choice out of hand, however, came as a shock, especially to Gwilt. The architect, who entered into a public spat with the council chairman, Mr Holme Sumner MP, never forgot and never forgave the snub.

When a second edition of the *Equilibrium* was published in 1826, he ensured an engraving of his London Bridge design was added to the book's frontispiece as a rebuke to the City. After his death, the topic was still considered such a stain on the family honour that his son, Sebastian, raised it in a memorial address, delivered to the Royal Institute of British Architects in February 1864. He complained that his father had been 'deprived of the reward he so justly merited', adding, with some venom, that this 'cannot now be ever but a subject of regret, whenever the present building is beheld'. 'The present building', so dismal to Gwilt Jnr in 1864, was, of course, to stand over the Thames for another century.

That bridge, however, was not – technically – even the second choice.

As an alternative more agreeable to everyone concerned, a five-arch bridge by Charles Fowler was the next selection. Fowler was a former assistant to David Laing, one of John Soane's pupils, and came to the competition fresh from completing the new Court of Bankruptcy on Basinghall Street in the City – a building long since lost to us, but thought, admittedly somewhat opaquely, 'handsome and large' by the *Leisure Hour* periodical in 1858.

His principal standing contribution to London is his market hall in the Piazza at Covent Garden. With its central arcade, long narrow courts, shops, and surrounding Greek Doric colonnade, it was the progenitor of all London markets of this type, and for over 140 years its air was heady with the scent of fruit and flowers. Fowler would go on to provide a slightly grander sibling at Hungerford

Market, the shopping ground just a stone's throw from the Strand, but that was demolished with the construction of Charing Cross Station in 1860.

In his influential post-war book, *Georgian London*, the architectural historian John Summerton maintained that Fowler's 'original sense of structure and planning' placed him 'alongside engineers like Rennie and Telford'. One wonders how Fowler would have responded to such a comparison after learning that the City Corporation had rejected his prize-winning study for London Bridge in favour of another drawn up by John Rennie. That Rennie was, by this juncture, also dead, having passed away on 4 October 1821, can surely only have added to the insult. The living, particularly in the highly competitive field of architecture, can perhaps be forgiven for muscling in on a deal. To be gazumped by someone from beyond the grave, though, offers up a quite frightening world where every fleeting shadow is a plausible assailant/available for hire.

In reality, Rennie had submitted his design to the City Corporation 'on spec' the previous year. At that point the engineer had still been alive, if increasingly unwell, and was deeply involved with the Corporation's architectural decision-making over the bridge, having just been dispatched to survey the Thames on their behalf. That Rennie, the ultimate insider, had his design slipped in on the sly seems to rather undermine the whole purpose of the open competition.

But then who better to design London Bridge than someone

who has the most up-to-date and intimate knowledge of the terrain and the Corporation's requirements?

And who wouldn't want to at least consider a bridge by John Rennie? The engineer was a giant in the field, and in every sense: he was six feet four with a proud Easter Island idol slab of a head topping off a robust frame. Like his almost exact contemporary and compatriot Thomas Telford, Rennie's life (and work) spans the transformation of Britain from a largely agricultural nation into a mainly industrial one.

If Samuel Smiles is to be believed – and, aside from Dickens, no rags are raggier than in any of the rags-to-riches tales that fill his book *The Lives of the Engineers* – at the time of Rennie's birth in 1761 the turnip remained a recent delicacy in his native Phantassie. A farming hamlet of thatched mud cottages sitting on a desolate moor twenty miles outside Edinburgh, this remote backwater was swept mercilessly into the eighteenth century two years later, when improvements to the nearby post-road brought the first stage-coaches to London past their door. Departing once a month, these coaches put the English capital a mere eleven to eighteen days within reach of Edinburgh. Though Rennie would not live to see the railway age, the gulf between this world and the one he departed in 1821 of factories, canals, iron bridges, wet docks, macadamised road surfaces and steamboats journeying from the Clyde to the Thames was more extreme than we can possibly comprehend now.

With the exception of the boats, off limits owing to a contract Rennie signed with James Watt agreeing never to venture into the field of steam, smears of his meaty fingerprints can be detected on each and every one of those other innovations – and much else besides. Ball bearings. The gantry crane. Iron-wheeled gears. The full list of Rennie's diverse contributions to the unfolding Industrial Revolution would run to several pages.

Commencing at 5 a.m. most mornings and remaining 'incessantly occupied' until gone midnight, Rennie almost certainly worked himself to death. He is only known to have taken one holiday in his entire career. That was a month on the Continent in 1816 in the company of James Watt's son, James Jnr, and seemingly consisted of seeking out the docks, harbours, canals and bridges erected during Napoleon's reign. As a young man capable of hoisting a third of a hundredweight aloft on his middle finger and thinking nothing of walking forty or more miles in a day, Rennie's body was shattered at fifty. But congenitally incapable of reducing his punishing schedule, he continued to be industrious to the last, writing a final business letter only five days before his death.

Smiles states that 'at six years old his best-loved toys were his knife, hammer, chisel, and saw' and, other than offering up a somewhat alarming snapshot of what passed for innocent childhood entertainment in the two centuries before Lego (and Health and Safety legislation), this detail stands as a portent for Rennie's almost singular obsession with tinkering around with things. If not fully the dour Scot his Presbyterian background and that work rate might suggest, enjoying, by all accounts, company, tall stories and good talk, he had few, if any, real interests outside engineering.

He liked to collect old books, but this was a rare indulgence in an existence markedly devoid of indulgences. Knockabout fun did not really fit into his life, but then neither did avowed Puritanism. For Rennie the greatest pleasure was to be derived from whittling away on a problem and coming up with a solution.

Always serious, and honest about money, his rates, at seven guineas a day, were the highest of any consulting engineer of the period, and he never knowingly under-quoted to gain a commission, usually doing quite the reverse in fact. But Rennie was often content to let others profit from a technical advance that had originated from his fecund brain. Shown a canny method for retaining walls for docks, the Inspector General of Naval Works, Sir Samuel Bentham, falling closer in step with Hobbes than his 'greater good' utilitarian brother Jeremy, patented it when Rennie failed to. Similarly, Rennie was building macadamised roads a good year before their namesake, John McAdam, perfected and assumed ownership of the technique.

Even the now notorious dispute between Rennie and his one-time collaborator Robert Stevenson, grandfather of *Treasure Island* author Robert Louis Stevenson, over the design of the Bell Rock Lighthouse raged with far greater intensity after his death. Erected some eleven miles off the coast of Angus on a craggy face of rock that for centuries had wrecked countless ships on its serrated edges, the lighthouse, standing a hundred feet high in white granite and seemingly unsupported in the middle of the ferocious waves of the North Sea, was justly regarded as a major feat of engineering on its completion in 1810. The initial plan for the lighthouse had stemmed from Stevenson, who was subsequently appointed as the resident engineer on the project, but Rennie, at the behest of the Northern Lighthouse Board, was brought in as the consulting engineer and certainly had a significant influence on the final design – though he remained in London during most of its construction. Stevenson, though, was adamant in denying Rennie's contribution.

The matter certainly rankled Rennie all the while he lived; in a rare public display of temper, Rennie once took umbrage at a blithe suggestion from a contractor that the two Scots might like to work together again. But it was the publication in 1824 of a book on the building of the lighthouse by Stevenson that verged on Stalinist for airbrushing Rennie out of the picture that stoked a feud. Rennie, dead for three years by then, was unable to counter with his own version of events. But his sons, George and John Jnr, recognised a slight when they saw one, and returned fire. In time they recruited Samuel Smiles to their cause, kindling a clannish battle that resulted in each of the two families spilling as much ink as the Campbells and MacDonalds had blood at Glencoe.

When it came to London Bridge, it was Rennie's sons who, with nepotistic zeal, ensured their father's design was built – a design for a noble, classical granite bridge of five semi-elliptical arches, two of 130 feet, two of 140 feet and a central arch of 152 feet and six inches. John Jnr gained the appointment from the City to act as chief engineer on the project. This was, in many respects, a mistake. It was George who had calculated the dimensions for the arches, voussoirs, piers and abutments for the new bridge; Rennie Snr had in fact been laid up with gout for much of the period when his Thames report was supposed to be made, so George had stepped into the breach. The 'Rennie bridge' was, then, in effect a product of the dynasty rather than the patriarch. But when the City came to approve it, George was engaged on another crossing for the Crown at Staines. The baton therefore passed to John Jnr, who, while a capable enough engineer, was 'not', in the judgement of H. L. Hopkins, 'a bridge man'. Hopkins cites John Jnr's memoirs as evidence of this, pointing out that while he gives detailed impressions of the various docks and harbours he encountered on a tour of France, Greece and Italy, not a single bridge was worth a mention. It is not beyond the bounds of possibility that he simply didn't see any interesting bridges on that particular trip. Perhaps he was so bowled over by the magnificence of the docks and harbours, that the bridges could never compete, their arches appearing as cold shoulders turned to him in comparison with the sensuous inviting lines of the Continent's ship-handling facilities. But it is, admittedly, a tad unlikely.

Whatever John Jnr's predilections, it is fair to say that his older brother George was certainly the more dedicated, if not also the more talented, engineer. Though categorised as 'a cripple', in the grimly derisive language of an age when left-handedness continued to be viewed as a biological abomination, George seems to have inherited his father's appetite – and stamina – for graft. He worked closely alongside the old man on his other Thames bridges, Waterloo in 1817 and Southwark in 1819, and went on to equip the Serpentine in Hyde Park with the serene five-arch Bath stone crossing that stands there to this day; although its keystones – those Trivial Pursuit pie-type wedge blocks that have formed the basis for masonry arches since Roman times – done up as engorged treble-clef-esque scrolls, remain an exasperatingly tacky decoration that despite a Grade II listing invite chiselling off even now.

Still, construction of this bridge, as a contract obtained by the family firm, was overseen by both brothers. And in the wake of their father's death, these siblings did forge an almost invincible business partnership, an alliance that was often profitable for its pragmatism with regard to their different engineering interests and abilities – a late move into manufacturing had George, for example, generating the first biscuit-making machine.*

Nevertheless, it is plain that their dealings with each other were far from easy. Their characters and temperaments were as wildly differing as Esau and Jacob. George was a staunch Presbyterian believing earnestly in the virtues of temperate habits, self-discipline and, of course, hard work. John Jnr, on the other hand, and in glaring contrast to his late father, wasn't averse to leisure or above acquiring some of the shinier trappings of position and wealth. These opposing aspects of their personalities were to come to the fore on London Bridge, putting an enormous strain on their working relationship.

What was to become the most contentious issue for George, though, was John Jnr's subsequent acceptance of a knighthood for his services on London Bridge. Casting his mind back to 1817, George, and practically everyone else, could immediately recall a similar bauble being dangled in front of their late father. It was 18 June, and the second anniversary of the Battle of Waterloo. The Prince Regent, who had assumed control of the throne in the year

---

* The significance of London Bridge to the brothers' subsequent reputation is borne out by an entry from the novelist Sir Walter Scott's journals. On 26 January 1827, Scott wrote: 'was introduced to young Mr Rennie, or he to me, by James Hall, a genteel-looking young man, and speaks well. He was called into public notice by having, many years before, made a draught of a plan of his father's for London Bridge. It was sought for when the building was really about to take place, and the assistance which young Mr Rennie gave to render it useful raised his character so high that his brother and he are now in first-rate practice as civil engineers.'

the foundation stone was laid, was presiding over the opening of what until only a few months earlier had been called the Strand Bridge. Its construction had taken six years and considerable expense. All of which appeared more than justified on this warm afternoon with sunny feelings of patriotism mingling with admiration for the bridge's lofty elegance – itself, naturally, a sturdy totem of British ingenuity in Cornish and Aberdeen granite, and decked for the occasion with bunting and flags.

Towering high above the Thames, it had a total length of 245 feet with approaches and causeways that carried it from the Strand to within spitting distance of the Old Surrey Theatre. The main roadway, virtually level on the summit of its nine semi-elliptical arches, ran for over 120 feet. The whole bridge was purposely intended to complement Sir William Chambers' monumental Somerset House, a building oozing Parisian neoclassicalism with its Corinthian pavilions, arched gateway and large interior court, and whose southern terrace was still lapped at by the as yet un-embanked Thames.

Billed in advance as a 'work of great stability and magnificence', Rennie's Waterloo Bridge was pronounced 'the noblest bridge in the world' by the Venetian sculptor Canova, who was enraptured by the concision of its Grecian Doric columns and cornice balustrade. The Prince Regent was no less impressed. And as he stood admiring the cut of its gib through the protracted blessings and toasts, while most likely already half-cut from his perennial regimen of laudanum, wine and brandy, he was gripped by a single idea. There beside him was the Duke of Wellington. Thin as a breadstick, he only served to make the prince seem more grotesquely corpulent, doughy and powdered: a revolting, sweaty iced bun of a man. Beyond the duke, and the other predictable dignitaries (the Duke of York, lords, ladies, mayors) were a smattering of the officers decorated for their valour at Waterloo. In time, the prince would become increasingly fond of regaling dinner guests at the Marine Pavilion in Brighton with tales of his own prowess on the battlefield against Napoleon (fantasies embellished, much like the pavilion itself, with every passing year). But here, the regent was in a more magnanimous (and less delusional) frame of mind. Evidently feeling credit should be given where credit was due, at least on this glorious ceremonial occasion, he decided then and there to knight the bridge's designer. If the bridge was worthy of honouring the nation's greatest military victory to date, its name authorised by an Act of Parliament in the previous year, then surely, the prince reasoned, it followed that John Rennie deserved to be ennobled.

Rennie, apparently privately horrified at the idea of receiving an honour from such a dishonourable regent, pleaded diffidence and tactfully succeeded in batting the suggestion away without upsetting the prince. In a letter to a friend that conveys his unease at the situation, he wrote, 'I had a hard business to escape a knighthood at the opening.'

But when the regent's successor and Rennie's younger son were to meet at the ribbon cutting of London Bridge some years on it was to be quite another matter – leading a distant member of the Rennie clan to comment somewhat caustically that 'whereas his father was interested in the building of memorable constructions', John Jnr was 'more interested in proffering the shoulder for accolades'. A sentiment it is plain George shared.

There was another Thames bridge for all the Rennies to complete before then, however. Ever the proficient multitasker (to use the modern jargon), while at work on Waterloo John Rennie was also engaged on two other bridges, one at Rochester and the other at Southwark – along, incidentally, with building a sewer for Regent's Park and preparing a report on a steam-driven paper-making machine for the Bank of England.

Rennie Snr has been described, quite accurately, as one of the last great stone men and with Vauxhall Bridge in 1816, and in circumstances thick with notes furtively passed and hands shaken in club rooms over late-night brandies, his stone design was hastily dumped in favour of a cheaper iron one, largely the work of James Walker. But Rennie did design several cast-iron bridges, beginning in the 1790s.

One of his most successful was Southwark Bridge, completed in 1819. This bridge was to cross the Thames at one of the narrowest and most congested parts of the river between Blackfriars and London Bridge. The Corporation of London and the Conservators of the Thames had opposed its construction, contending that it would obstruct navigation. To satisfy their objections, Rennie had to devise a bridge that allowed traffic to pass as freely as possible, and to achieve that he needed a structure with high broad arches and as few piers as practical. So, iron seemed the only solution. Using cast-iron girders to form the lengthy spans required, Rennie was eventually able to deliver a bridge of three arches and just two stone piers and abutments. At 240 feet, its central arch, four feet longer than Wilson's Wearmouth Bridge, was to be the longest span ever constructed in cast iron. The whole bridge was comprised of some 3,732 tons of iron. Unfortunately its contractors, Walkers of Rotherham, the iron founders who'd supplied Thomas Paine over two decades earlier, again had problems producing castings on the scale Rennie requested, and this, coupled with other difficulties over Southwark Bridge, plunged the company into bankruptcy.

The abutments and piers that served as the structural ballast to all that iron, meanwhile, were fashioned from gigantic blocks of Peterhead granite. These were personally selected in Aberdeenshire by John Jnr, who also produced working drawings for the bridge. However, already displaying an ease with idleness that would recur throughout his career, he was to duck out of the project before its end. Feigning exhaustion, he departed for a holiday in Belgium, leaving his father and brother to continue with the bridge while he toured the battlefields of Waterloo.

As a design, Rennie's Southwark Bridge proved influential, serving as the template for scores of the first generation of cast-iron railway bridges. Nearly fifty years after its construction the railway pioneer Robert Stephenson remained unsparing in his praise, judging this example of arch construction 'confessedly unrivalled as regards its colossal proportions, its architectural effect and the general simplicity and massive character of its details'.

And it lasted for ninety years. But unfortunately the character of its details was not the only thing that was massive. In the view of modern-day engineers, Rennie, perhaps erring on the safe side, is believed to have made the bridge 'unnecessarily heavy'. Among a catalogue of other faults, some minor, others fatal, was a failure to lure road traffic away from the bridge's immediate neighbours, Blackfriars and London Bridge. Southwark's roadway, at twenty-eight feet, was rather narrow, with poor approaches that left it inadequately plumbed into the main thoroughfares on either bank.

By contrast, when it came to the new London Bridge, the approach roads would cost close to three times as much as the whole bridge itself. To raise the £1,840,438 needed to pay for this work alone, the Tory government, pushed kicking and screaming through the voting lobbies by their prime minister, the Duke of Wellington, took the then almost unprecedented step of placing an additional tax on coal.*

* Wellington was not a popular PM. His stubborn defence of an almost in-defensible system of political representation, which left increasingly populous urban cities like Manchester, Leeds and Birmingham without a single elected MP while Cornwall returned forty-four members, might have led to the collapse of his administration. His home, Apsley House, would be pelted with stones by disgruntled Londoners, its windows fitted with iron shutters and its rooms protected by an armed guard. The lord mayor's banquet would be cancelled in case its pomp and pageantry inflamed an already angry populous to run riot in the capital. And the duke himself would become the object of popular hatred, narrowly avoiding at least one attack by a mob, and openly hissed at as he made his way about the streets. But to the cause of a new London Bridge, Wellington was unstintingly and enthusiastically loyal. Throughout the turmoils of 1830, the duke was often to be found down by the river inspecting the works in progress. Riding up on his horse at around five or six in the morning on warmer days, lean-framed, five feet eight, ruddy-faced, hook-nosed, and invariably clad in a blue tailcoat, he cut an instantly recognisable, if for the moment far from revered, figure. His

Part of the origin of this extraordinary outlay was the insistence by the Corporation of London that the new bridge be sited upstream from the old one. This idea stemmed from the not unreasonable anxiety that if London Bridge was closed for rebuilding, the Square Mile would be reduced to a quivering mass of inert carts and carriages, its blocked streets soon running knee-deep in horse dung. To avoid such a calamity, the ancient bridge would stay open, while the new one arose by its side. Their reasoning was sound enough. Back in 1758, when George Dance the Elder was widening de Colechurch's bridge and ridding it of its motley assortment of houses and shops, he had built a temporary wooden bridge alongside the main bridge, shutting the latter so that the work could progress without being disturbed by traffic. But on the evening of 11 April that year, someone – and the only obvious candidate is one (or more) of the watermen – set fire to the wooden bridge. The City was suddenly separated from Southwark for the first time since the Great Stone Gate and two arches of the old bridge had collapsed in 1437 and, for a while, the capital was left solely reliant on boats to cross this part of the river. The City were adamant that they were not going through that kind of farrago again.

But this was not what John Rennie Snr had first planned. Under his initial proposal the new bridge was to have occupied exactly

abiding faith in a stratified British society, where property rights and en-lightened aristocratic patronage held sway, to some appeared as medieval and as dated as the Old London Bridge that was to be swept away. Its re-placement, however, was in many respects a Wellingtonian piece, as it was arguably not quite as modern as it needed to be.

the same spot as its predecessor, with a temporary crossing à la Dance the Elder's mopping up the traffic in between. While possibly causing Londoners greater inconvenience during construction and putting them again at the mercy of arsonist watermen, this scheme had several advantages. In preserving the line from Fish Street Hill that dated from Peter de Colechurch's time, less of the fabric of the City would be disturbed. Accordingly, less would therefore need to be spent on buying up properties in order to lay new roads or divert old ones.

There were also topographical advantages to the existing site – de Colechurch's bridge stood on slightly higher ground. Equally, building in a tidal river is nowhere near as easy as building on land, regardless of how taxing problems such as gravity, subsidence, etc.

can be. You can't simply plonk one bridge down next to another in the cheek-by-jowl style that is characteristic of the London streetscape to this day without affecting the waterway as a whole. The builder *sur le fleuve* is locked into a much more fiercely Sisyphean battle with their working environment than their peers on terra firma. To begin with, the resistant current, rather like the ceaselessly murdering sardine can in the *Terminator* films, is constantly reinvigorated by the arrival of each fresh object in its path. If, in the case of the immediate environs of London Bridge, that river is already partially blocked, then adding further obstructions can unleash quite terrifyingly volatile rushes of water. For bridge engineers in the opening decades of the nineteenth century, even armed with superior technology than their forebears, construction in such situations remained a perilous business. Therefore to keep the destructive forces of the Thames at a minimum, John Rennie had wanted to clear the old bridge away and leave the river to settle before embarking on the arduous task of erecting his new crossing in the stream.

Despite expressing sizeable misgivings, and protesting that the City's plan would result in 'considerable difficulty, risk and extra expense', John Jnr, perhaps lacking his father's clout, was left with no real alternative but to yield to the Corporation's demands. Aided by George, his first major headache was to rejig the design to fit this new location, or perhaps more accurately, to rejig the location to accommodate the design, since substantial and costly redevelopments of both banks would prove necessary in the end. On the north bank a completely new road, King William Street, tracking from the Royal Exchange to the bridge, was laid out, and on the south Borough High Street widened and realigned. The Old Fishmongers Hall was demolished and an arch over Thames Street incorporated into the final design on the north bank. The bridge's roadway was also widened from forty-eight to fifty-four feet, adding another £46,000 to a bill that would eventually nudge £2,556,170 – the equivalent of £126,504,853 in 2012.

Work commenced on 15 March 1824, and the foundation stone was laid with a ceremony conducted forty feet below the river, inside the first pier cofferdam on the Surrey side, on 15 June 1825. According to one contemporary observer, the interior of this cofferdam, a massive elliptical timber chamber pumped dry by steam engines, was 'fitted up with great taste like an amphitheatre, with seats all round, the whole being covered at top with a handsome coloured canvas awning adorned with numerous flags of all nations'. The guest of honour was the king's brother, Prince Frederick, *the* 'Grand Old' Duke of York whose abortive military campaign in Holland in 1794 supposedly gave rise to the nursery rhyme. That the duke, on this occasion, had to march with the lord mayor and the City aldermen, down into the heart of the cofferdam and then back up again, must have produced a smirk or fifty among the assembled masses in Southwark.

But the artful gaiety of the official pageant couldn't entirely mask the arduousness of the undertaking at hand, which at this stage involved labouring in depths of twenty-five to thirty feet at low tide and on a hard bed of treacherously alluvial clay. Seven and a half years would pass and over forty lives would be lost before it was finished – though that was a quarter of the time its predecessor, which was two and a half times narrower, had taken to build. And that old bridge, as Rennie Snr (and Jnr) had feared, proved a constant thorn in their side – and arguably more than held its own in bumping up the casualty rate. From the loose stones that clustered around its decayed piers, hazardous as unexploded mines, to the almighty torrents its restricted waterways unleashed, it appeared almost booby-trapped to thwart its usurpers' every move. Among those injured during the bridge's construction was John Rennie Jnr himself, who slipped on a beam while inspecting one of the piers and fell headlong into the cofferdam. Fortunately, he caught his foot on a nail, which pitched him on to an inclined plank that cushioned his descent. But he struck his head on some masonry on the way

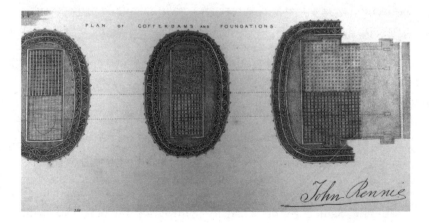

down and was left concussed and bloodied. 'My whole system,' he later reflected, 'got such a severe shaking, that I did not recover thoroughly until nearly ten years afterwards, and I carried on my large professional business with the greatest of difficulty.'

Signing on for eight contracts for building the new bridge (and removing the old one) between March 1824 and June 1830 were the independent firm of Jolliffe and Banks, whose prestigious CV came burnished with their efforts for John Rennie on the bridges at Southwark and Waterloo. This company was formed from an unlikely, if lucrative, partnership between a Yorkshire-born merchant seaman turned navvy, Edward Banks, and the Reverend William Jolliffe, the MP for Petersfield in Hampshire who abandoned thoughts of holy office for a significantly more material career. The pair met in the early 1800s at Merstham in Surrey, where Jolliffe lived in the splendour of his Great House, and Banks was engaged on the Croydon, Merstham & Godstone Iron Railway. They would pool their resources to build the Court House in Croydon before carving out a formidable reputation as contractors for hire and making aquatic projects such as the Eau Brink Cut, the Sheerness Docks and the embankments at Cardiff Bay their speciality. (That Peter de Colechurch, like many medieval bridge builders, was a cleric provides a continuum of sorts between the construction of the two spans. Though judging from the damage the earlier crossing attempted to inflict on its successor, de Colechurch could be taken to be chastising Jolliffe for failing to heed his prior spiritual vocation.)

Rennie, Samuel Smiles liked to claim, 'built for posterity', and with London Bridge, his son, erecting a tribute to his father, went all out for a lasting monument. At a colossal 130,000 tons, the new structure was to the heaviest London had ever seen – a size-twelve hobnail boot of a bridge, pounding the clay substrata with all its might. Its outer stonework was fashioned in a white-grey granite from Haytor in Devon and Aberdeen in Scotland, with a few lumps from Cornwall thrown in by Jolliffe and Banks when supplies from the former ran low. Beefing up that was an inner core of hard Yorkshire gritstone from Bramley Fall, the quarry later to supply Philip Hardwick with the materials for his Doric propylaeum at Euston Station in 1837. And other connections abound between these two 'arches'. Both were about providing stately entrances to (and exits from) London and both, as we shall see, were finally, and symbolically, removed from the capital in the 1960s.*

---

* In an autobiography, published in 1875, John Jnr would wax lyrical about his school days at Dr Greenlaw's Syon House Academy in Isleworth. Then aged about twelve or thirteen, one of his fellow pupils was Percy Bysshe Shelley. He recalled that the young poet was subject to 'violent paroxysms of rage', had a penchant for explosive pranks with gunpowder, and was 'rather effeminate . . . exceedingly animated' with an imagination 'always roving upon something romantic and extraordinary'. In the words of biographer Richard Holmes, 'Shelley found little companionship at Syon House', and later drew on his unhappy experiences at the school in 'The Revolt of Islam' – a poetic indictment of tyranny composed while John Jnr was toiling alongside his father on Waterloo Bridge, or more probably, recuperating in Belgium. And although hypochondria might well have been an area of common ground, Rennie and Shelley were never destined to be friends. Nor, as far as can be ascertained, did they ever encounter one another again as adults. And yet, the image from Shelley's 'Ozymandias' of a chunk of long superfluous imperial granite in a barren desert, the supreme cliché that it has become, does seem unavoidably, and rather more precisely, prophetic in this instance. Just to add to the 'Look on my works, ye Mighty, and despair' aspect, Rennie Snr was buried in St Paul's Cathedral under a rectangular prism of polished granite – the same substance used for 'his' posthumous London Bridge – and engraved on the stone was the epitaph 'THE TRUE MONUMENTS of PUBLIC MERIT Waterloo – Southwark – Bridges'. Neither of which were to endure.

CHAPTER 5

Arc de Triomphe

The new London Bridge was opened on 1 August 1831 in a spectacle that John Jnr judged 'perhaps . . . the most brilliant of any that had taken place for fully a century'. Viewed as an event of national importance, at a moment when the country was in turmoil over electoral reform, the ceremony was also something of a dry run for King William IV's coronation only a month later, an affair modest to the point of cheeseparing in comparison with George IV's extravagant fiasco a decade earlier. *The Times*, grappling for the pulse of the nation, devoted an expansive four and a half columns of their four pages to the bridge's opening. It recorded that future Tory prime minister, Sir Robert Peel, who had opposed the first Reform Bill, 'was ill-received by some of the company who gave a tolerably intelligent opinion of his late conduct by hissing'. This, however, turned out to be a rare note of discontent in the proceedings. The public who filled the streets and jammed themselves into the buildings, wharfs and warehouses beside the river, were mostly there to gawp at their new(ish) monarch, and treated him and his queen to a cordial display of affection. Palpable relief that the old fat profligate one with the suppurating legs, who'd requested a copy of the *Racing Calendar* on his deathbed, was finally out of the picture only contributed to the gestures of bonhomie shown to his successor throughout the day.

Escorted by the Life and Royal Horse Guards, King William and Queen Adelaide processed to Somerset House in a fleet of twelve carriages. There the Royal Standard was raised, and cannons fired and the party boarded a barge to cruise along the Thames to the new bridge. This river trip, laden with nautical symbolism, was especially welcomed by the new king. William genuinely hoped to redeem the sullied institution of the English monarchy by stamping his own personal – and much more personable – identity on the role. And William's sense of himself as a navy man was fundamental to that identity.

After watching him at a ball held by the Duke of Wellington about this time, the American diplomat and writer Washington Irving noted, not unkindly, that William IV had 'an easy and natural way of wiping his nose with the back of his forefinger'. A 'relic', Irving fancied, 'of his middy habits' (i.e. naval duties). Later affectionately known as 'the Sailor King', William had been packed off to sea as a teenager by his parents, after forming the first in a line of unsuitable romantic attachments. And, throughout life, this one-time Lord High Admiral propagated what the Whig politician and assiduous chronicler of the era Thomas Creevey dubbed 'a Wapping air'.

Happiest messing around in boats (and barges), and often encountered by his subjects ambling unsteadily about on the saline-lashed timbers of Brighton's Chain Pier, William had really never expected to become king. As the third son of George III and Queen

Charlotte, an heir (George) and a spare (Frederick) stood between him and the throne. Accordingly, there was less risk to the House of Hanover in pressing him into the navy early, where character-building active duty might also entail meeting a stray cannonball or a shipwreck – or a deadly combination of the two.

Exactly fifty years prior to the opening of London Bridge, and then aged only sixteen, William was dispatched to America during the Revolutionary War. Sailing from Gibraltar on the *Prince George* under Admiral Digby, he'd arrived in Sandy Hook, New York, in August 1781. While across the Hudson, New Jersey, perhaps chomping at the bit to enjoy the same taxation rights as its Channel Island forebears, had fallen to the rebels, New York remained committed to the Crown. The prince's presence would, it was hoped, serve as a backbone stiffener for loyalist morale. And if William was not particularly taken with the Big Apple, damning its streets, which he wandered quite freely, as 'Dutch . . . narrow and very ill-paved', the residents, appreciating the effort, went out of their way to demonstrate their enthusiasm for his visit. News of this royal representation inevitably reached the continental forces over the water and one of their leading officers, Colonel Odgen, hatched a plan to sneak over from New Jersey in whaleboats and kidnap the prince and the admiral. This audacious scheme, incredibly enough, received the full backing of George Washington. But rumours of the plot leaked, scuppering any attempt on the prince in New York in the end. Years later, and admittedly at a diplomatic dinner with the wine and insincerity no doubt flowing in large measures, the king was to declare that it had been a matter of enormous regret that he had not 'been born a free, independent American, so much did he respect that nation, which had given birth to Washington, the greatest man that ever lived'.

Back on the Thames, it's doubtful that America – this new bridge's final resting place – so much as crossed William's mind, as the barge carried him under one of the crossing's four broad stone archways before depositing its regal cargo at the foot of a huge tented pavilion at the City side. That tent was festooned with 'flags, shields and standards of armies that had formerly waved over almost every civilised country in the world' – including that of America. And further adding to the air of international jollity, the crowds, patiently waiting for over two hours, had been entertained by a troupe of German minstrels, 'the Altonian Siffleur' Herr von Joel – a birdsong imitator, the linnet his *pièce de résistance*, once criticised for blowing his 'garlicked breath' into the faces of visitors to Vauxhall Gardens – and a 'still more celebrated performer' whose name and extraction have been left to the imagination, who was lauded by *The Times* for demonstrating an 'independence of all musical instrument makes by playing tunes upon his chin with his fists'. The king's arrival was marked by a rather more traditional performance from a military band on an adjacent barge, its martial tones enhanced by twenty-one brass cannons firing a salute. Speeches made and the contentious knighthood conferred on John Jnr, the monarch and his ministers, the lord mayor and representatives from the Corporation strode the length of the bridge. Upon reaching the Southwark end, they threw commemorative medals into the hordes on the south bank, and then watched 'a balloon ascension by two aeronauts Mr Green and Mr Crawshay'.

Green, like Herr von Joel, was a familiar sight at Vauxhall Gardens and since his balloon was powered by coal gas he was perhaps no less offensive to the nose. But the man dubbed 'the Father of English Aeronautics' seems to have enjoyed a monopoly on major public events in this period, his ubiquity at regal celebrations, in particular, casting him as the Elton John of the early nineteenth century. He had, for instance, performed at George IV's coronation. Despite this, his dream of making the first flight across the Atlantic in a balloon, a journey he suggested to *The Times* could easily 'be performed in three or four days', floundered through lack of financial support.

Once the ballooning display was over, the entourage returned to the tent at the City end and the royal party sat down to 'a cold collation' with 2,000 guests accompanied by 'extremely good wines . . . at a banquet that was conducted on a scale of profuseness that was remarkable even in civic feasts'. At 6 p.m., the king and queen rose to another gun salute and clambered back on to the barge for their return journey, the river by this time 'covered with boats filled with gaily dressed people'.

The day was judged a triumph with *The Times* applauding it as 'one of the most gorgeous festivals in the annals of the metropolis'.

But barely a month after the opening, Peter Jeffreys, a cheesemaker at 81 Cheapside, presented a petition to Parliament stating that the new London Bridge was falling down. Though denounced by John

Jnr as the work of 'one of those active, intelligent persons, who are always interfering in matters which do not concern them', and possibly fuelled by personal enmity over an unsettled claim for compensation relating to the new approach roads, Jeffreys' allegations were not completely unfounded.

Like J. F. Sebastian, the Methuselah Syndrome-afflicted geek in the film *Blade Runner*, the new bridge appeared to be ageing at an unnervingly accelerated rate. A few of its arch-stones were already veined with cracks. Much more worryingly, parts of the bridge, most noticeably two piers on the south abutments and one of its flights of steps, had slumped somewhat, lending the structure a drunken-sailor gait that rolled to the south-east by two or three inches in places. It also became fast apparent that there were glaring irregularities between the heights of some of the piers. The first pier was found to be over six and a half inches higher than the third.

As the full-scale riots in Bristol that autumn over the sluggish pace of parliamentary reform demonstrated, this remained, in many respects, a crooked age. And as deformed as it was, the new bridge was arguably no worse than similar stone crossings at Neuilly near Paris or those at Gloucester, Totnes, Kew, Richmond or, even closer, at Westminster. Nevertheless Jeffreys' petition raised legitimate concerns about its stability. With most of the old bridge still hunkered in the river, and, although now minus two arches and its waterwheels, continuing to do its damndest to hold back the tide, there were fears that with its removal a resurgent Thames might simply wash its heir away. By October a commission was appointed to undertake a thorough investigation of the state of the new bridge.

It was comprised of Thomas Telford, James Walker, the chief designer of Vauxhall Bridge, and Tierney Clark, creator of the first suspension bridge over the Thames at Hammersmith in 1827. Their final report, based on extensive field studies and a series of hearings with the bridge's engineers and contractors, was presented to Parliament on 17 November 1831 and printed the following January. This concluded that the bridge was structurally sound. They found 'no pains' seemed to have been 'spared, in regards to the materials and worksmanship' and went so far as to salute the parapet of the bridge 'as perfect a specimen of granite work as any have ever seen'. The cracks in the arch-stones were attributed to 'imperfections in the particular stones' that they believed could not have been detected before they were in situ. The panel were equally forgiving when it came to the sunken steps and uneven piers. These were undoubtedly caused by 'inaccuracy in levelling and setting out the works' for the foundations. But such flaws were understandable as the clay bed had been extremely hard going and was 'several feet higher at the west than at the east end'. As there were no signs of further subsidence, the committee urged the contractors to press on with the demolition of the old bridge.

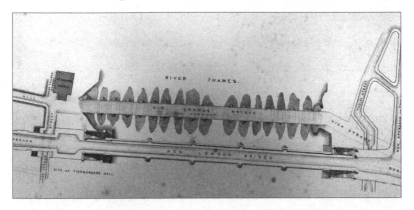

This gateway into the City for over 600 years, a stalwart witness to London as it had grown from a dunghill on the fringes of Europe to one of the most important cities in the world, was finally surplus to requirements. Its arches and piers had been patched and repatched so often, it seemed almost inconceivable to some that it could ever go, deserted and half-demolished as it was. But go it did and with very little ceremony. Though as the stream of increasingly terse letters John Jnr dispatched to Jolliffe and Banks about progress (or the lack of it)* on the demolition well into 1833 illustrate, Peter de Colechurch's bridge was in no particular rush to leave. And who could blame it for that? While three of his opening nineteen arches – and the drawbridge – had been removed and seven completely rebuilt, half of its arches, if doubled in width and tarted up with

---

* 'I really must request and urge you to commence filling up the holes and level the bed of the River below the Old Bridge,' begins one typical missive.

fresh stone ribs, hailed from the priest–architect's days – as did a good number of its piers. That said, its life had been one of ceaseless repairs, the whole bridge being completely refaced with blocks of Portland ashlar between 1757 and 1762. Old London Bridge's biographer Gordon Home estimated that in 1831 around two-thirds of its stone, therefore, dated from the middle of the eighteenth century at the earliest, making the bulk of what was junked mere striplings of only seventy or eighty years of age. In the bridge's lifespan, these were the Porsche, dyed hair, ponytail and trophy blonde girlfriend accrued in that phase of desperate-to-stay-youthful late middle age.

A proportion of this spare masonry was used to fill holes left in the riverbed once the bridge's starlings had been dug out. Some was reserved to be deployed on new river walls or embankments. But a fair bit of it, perhaps aptly since the removal just about overlaps with the fictional time frame of Dickens' *Oliver Twist*, was carried off to places unspecified by persons unknown – that is: nicked. In 1832, the Bridge House Committee, alerted to the fact that five barges of rubble intended for embanking had been spirited away to Sheerness, the Kent coastal town where Banks and Jolliffe were handling much of the excess material, came close to dismissing John Jnr as the consulting engineer. That they would contemplate such an extreme action implies that literally tons of stone were going astray on his watch – and that they suspected some collusion on his part in the scam with Jolliffe and Banks.

This, coupled with legitimate sales, led to pieces of the bridge being scattered throughout the south-east, with estuary towns within an easy barge ride of London particularly rich in specimens. Like many a former city slicker retiring from the hassle and dirt of the big smoke, these stones embarked on new lives among the fresh air, green pastures and clear waters of the outer suburbs and beyond in newly formed seaside resorts. Until 1953, when they were swept away by the great east coast storm, two lengths of London Bridge's balustrade escorted trippers to Herne Bay on to its pier. A section of the bridge's Ashlar blocks faced a quay at Beaumont near Thorpe le Soken in Essex, and its stone walled the tower of the long since lost St James's Church at Warden on the Isle of Sheppey in Kent. At Greenhithe near Dartford, the City alderman and Bridge Committee member James Harmer finished off his Tudorbethan country house, Ingress Abbey, with Portland stock from the bridge. Snuffboxes and other trinkets and keepsakes, meanwhile, were turned from its pile wood.

The Pier and Gardens, Herne Bay. 28.

Not all of the bridge left the city entirely. To this day, a lump or two of London Bridge Portland can be spotted in the churchyard of St Magnus the Martyr on the City side of the bridge – its churchyard had been virtually the gangplank to the old bridge until 1831. On the fringes of Wandsworth Common in South London, then within living memory a haunt of highwaymen, a residence, unimaginatively known as 'the Stone House', was created from the bridge's medieval Kentish ragstone. When this was knocked down in 1909, the stone was recycled again for new properties on the site, most extensively on 49 Heathfield Road.

Of the fourteen alcoves foisted on the medieval span in the 1760s in slavish emulation of the kissing cubbies on Labelye's brand new Westminster Bridge, three stayed in the capital. Like a freed lifer not sure where to go next, one only got as far as Southwark, where it was used as a garden shelter for convalescing patients at Guy's Hospital. Two went east to Hackney, where they joined the scenic attractions of Victoria Park. A further two wound up as ornaments in the grounds of Stanwell House in East Sheen, Surrey. When this was demolished in 1937 to be replaced with flats, one of the alcoves was also destroyed, leaving just four in total standing today.

The casualness with which Jolliffe and Banks and Co. manifestly treated these architectural treasures reached outright callousness when their workers unearthed the remains of Peter de Colechurch. Where their direct professional ancestors had laid this brother of the bridge to rest under the floor of the lower chapel, reverently melding him with the fabric of a structure he never lived to see finished, these men seemingly tossed his bones into the Thames as thoughtlessly as a teenager encumbered with a freshly drained Coke can.*

*　　*　　*

The early Victorian period is often viewed as an epoch with a vast capacity for sentimentality. We only have to think of the mortally sick innocents that were such a staple of Charles Dickens' fiction serials. In February 1841, for example, American readers, anxious for news from England about the fate of Little Nell in *The Old Curiosity Shop*, gathered, handkerchiefs at the ready, to meet incoming boats on the quaysides of Boston and New York. But,

---

*　The Museum of London does hold a casket of bones that for many years were passed off as de Colechurch's remains. On closer inspection, however, these were revealed to hail from an assortment of different animals.

to borrow another Dickens title, these were, correspondingly, exceedingly hard times. And the opening decades of Victoria's reign would prove far meaner to the new bridge than any comparable period was to its predecessor. Partly, of course, this is because the whole pace of city life and technological advance was altering irrevocably.

Apart from pumping water out of the cofferdams, steam engines had played no role in the construction of Rennie's bridge. Jolliffe and Banks' men relied on hand-worked derricks and cranes to hoist the granite into position, using methods that would have been as familiar to their medieval forebears as trepanning. Yet within five years of its opening, locomotives would puff and clank their way to within 200 yards of the bridge. At a stroke, the creation of London Bridge Station on the south bank, the first railway terminus in the capital following a tentative start at Spa Road in Bermondsey, transformed the number of people flowing into the City over the bridge. What equally increased was the speed and volume of traffic going *under* the bridge. As the *Observer* newspaper reported in 1837 the public could now 'avail themselves of the river Thames as a highway, and secure a healthful, safe, quick and economical conveyance between Westminster Bridge, Hungerford Market and London Bridge, by means of commodious steamboats'.

This massive rise in traffic could never have been foreseen by the Rennies – Snr and Jnr. Their London Bridge was now an architectural throwback to the grandeur of eighteenth-century Paris, having originally been conceived for a city as yet untroubled by the horse-drawn omnibus, let alone steam trains. Consequently, its roadway was to become so clogged by 1853 that a proposal to widen the bridge was already under discussion.

In a report on the issue delivered to the Bridge House Estates five years on, John Jnr argued that any attempts at widening would be 'inadvisable'. City Architect Horace Jones was to disagree but later estimated that it would cost at least £25,000 to alter the bridge. The committee, baulking at this relatively trivial sum, opted, in the tradition of its much-patched forerunner, for a quick cheap fix instead. They rearranged the traffic into distinct lanes, restricting the heavier drays and wagons to outer roads nearer the kerb and allowing lighter vehicles to speed along on the inside track. This was a meagre response to the problem and after obfuscating for decades, they finally bowed to the inevitable and the bridge was widened with granite corbels – outer load-bearing brackets – in 1902.

In the meantime, John Wolfe Barry's twin-decked Tower Bridge had been thrown up on London Bridge's eastern side. This high Victorian Gothic confection replete with turrets and drawbridges was kitted out to emulate the toy-fort charms of the neighbouring Tower. An adjunct to the Port of London, which had become the busiest in the world and the hub of Victoria's empire, it owed its existence to the inevitable failure of London Bridge to keep pace with the city's expanding needs – a fact only further underlined by a plan mooted but rejected in the 1880s to build yet another span alongside it on the site of the original de Colechurch crossing.

Meanwhile, the removal of the Old London Bridge, combined

with the embanking of the Thames by the city in the 1850s and 1860s, allowed the tide to rampage further and faster upriver. With a tidal reach that was now only halted by the artificial barrier of Teddington Lock, the unfettered Thames had a merry time, darting into nooks and crannies far beyond its old ambit. Much as the neat parries of a rapier are harder to sidestep than lunges from a broadsword, this narrower and speedier river was a much deadlier proposition for all London's bridges to contend with. The new tide cut sharper and deeper into their foundations. Like that other killer of the age, TB, the deadly scour, in time, would carry off all the original spans at Blackfriars, Vauxhall, Westminster, Southwark and Waterloo.

PART TWO

CHAPTER 6

Swinging London

Wrecking balls, like packet mash potato or Saran Wrap, seem redolent of a past, one growing ever more distant, a past when the future would always be brighter. As familiar an addition to the landscape of the post-war era as gibbets were to the London of Johnson, their presence carried an equally weighty (and high-handed) ethical imperative. Lessons had to be learned, they said, as they swung about levelling the corrupt and the decrepit in the name of progress. One hangs in freeze-frame, like a sword of Damocles, above the title credits of the 1967 film *The London That Nobody Knows*. The same footage reappears in the documentary's final minutes, the image bookending the picture but also lurking, out of view but omnipresent, in every frame. The film was loosely based on a book by Geoffrey Fletcher, a Slade-trained sketch artist and journalist who monitored the changing face of the capital in an irascible if deeply felt column for the *Daily Telegraph* entitled 'London Day by Day'. Directed by Norman Cohen and scripted by Brian Comport, the cinematic version offered a peripatetic snapshot of the city in the throes of rapid new developments, and when King's Road and Carnaby Street were at their dandiest peaks. But simultaneously, whole tracts of the East End lay neglected and condemned.

James Mason, wearing a flat cap and tweed jacket, the mufti of hill walkers in his native Yorkshire, and armed with a rolled umbrella, is captured tramping, somewhat wearily, about a mostly crust-on-its-uppers London – a London whose streets look less swinging than scrofulous with bomb damage. Whole areas appear shabby with torched boxwood and putrefying cabbages and are roamed by packs of terrifying feral meths drinkers.* Foraging through the wreckage of the Bedford Music Hall theatre in Camden and the crowded stalls at Islington's Chapel Market, Mason is as quizzical and imperious as Sherlock Holmes. Meeting toothless down-on-their-lucks in a Salvation Army shelter in Whitechapel, one still rueing the consequences of the crash of 1929, he could be a visiting royal killing an hour before cutting the ribbon on a new civic centre elsewhere in the day. At times, his voice – *that* voice, honeyed as cognac, soft, melancholy, occasionally father-knows-best stentorian – becomes almost viscous with fatalistic languor.

But when the cavalcade of drunks, hawkers, escape artists and doughty cast-iron public lavatories, methane gas-powered street lamps and silk mercers' peeling shopfronts is eventually over, its end signalled by the return, like a pendulum, of the wrecking ball, it nevertheless remains a shock that Mason blithely posits the imminent destruction of nearly everything viewed in the previous forty-five minutes. Most of these buildings, he calmly asserts, are 'out of date, inefficient and taking up too much space'. There is

---

* Bob Stanley, writing about the film for the *Guardian* in 2003, summed it up best when he succinctly observed, 'London looks like a shit hole.'

'no need to be too sad about it', he adds, more hesitantly, 'after all, most of Victorian London was fairly hideous'.

Here Mason is simply voicing an opinion prevalent enough then to be regarded as a self-evident truth. For decades 'Victorian' and 'hideous' had been as close to inextricable in the collective consciousness as the words 'concrete' and 'monstrosity' would duly, and equally uncritically, become. Victorian architecture was enough of a joke by 1937 that P.G. Wodehouse, ensconced in Beverly Hills, could mock it in *Summer Moonshine*, a novel about a cash-strapped aristocrat lumbered with an ancestral pile whose nineteenth-century 'improvements' render it unsaleable. 'Whatever may be said in favour of the Victorians,' Wodehouse quips, 'it is pretty generally admitted that few of them were to be trusted within reach of a trowel and a pile of bricks.' But within *The London That Nobody Knows* traces of a subtle shift in attitudes to the era of bewhiskered table-leg coverers pokes through. Certainly the first stirrings of what would now be called 'gentrification' are clearly visible here. In Camden Town, Mason spies 'seedy terraces . . . coming up in the world, after years of neglect'. The camera, following a rag-and-bone merchant in a horse-drawn cart, a real-life Steptoe in a spotted neckerchief and battered felt hat, zeroes in on a stuccoed fascia that gleams like laundered tennis whites beside the urine-stained long johns of a neighbouring building. Pinned on its immaculate blackened front railings is an estate agent's board that exudes the air of a rosette awarded to a prize marrow at a garden fete.

One of the facets of the film version of Fletcher's book, and something that adds to its pleasingly dilatory tempo, is that Mason was obviously given leave to extemporise when the mood took him. Though, in a few instances, insouciant 'busking-it' seems a better definition, palpably in a section where the actor launches into a speech about London Bridge. The piece is delivered from the South Bank in front of Southwark Bridge. St Paul's, its dome enmeshed in scaffolding, hangs in the far right above his head, a waxing moon in the afternoon sky. The camera is facing upriver, leaving Mason with little option but to glance left and nod meaningfully in London Bridge's direction, these gestures supplemented by the odd cursory wave of his umbrella. 'Up to a few years ago there was a very real danger that London Bridge might fall down,' he states, emphatically, before becoming decidedly fuzzier on the details. 'Something to do with the riverbed being a bit soft,' he ventures, as if unable to recall the precise facts and/or the script. 'But they managed to prop it up,' he pipes, like a bedtime storyteller rushing to bring that evening's duties to an end. And then, after pausing for a millisecond, he signs off on the topic with the words: 'Successfully, I hope' – a line that only succeeds in sowing further doubts. We then abruptly move on to a comic sequence involving smashed eggs, a steamroller and some dubiously racist imitations of karate.*

But in 1967, London Bridge needed far more than James Mason's hopes to keep it propped up. Like so much else in the city at that point, its imminent removal was already a done deal. The decision to replace the Rennies' 1831 structure with a new crossing had, in fact, been agreed two years earlier by the Bridge House Committee. This piece of information, if in the public domain, seems to have enjoyed a profile nearly as low as a post-scandal John Profumo, though in the context of the 1960s, when fresh schemes were being unveiled practically hour by hour, that is not too surprising. Even seasoned commentators on London's architectural scene, men like Geoffrey Fletcher and Ian Nairn of The *Observer*, had a tough job keeping up with every demolition and speculation. As an indicator of the hectic rate with which old buildings were being torn down, when Ian Nairn's own gazetteer, *Nairn's London*, first appeared in 1966 its back cover warned purchasers that 'some of its entries are

---

* Groundwork, perhaps, for his forthcoming performance in *The Ying and Yang of Mr Go*.

already disappearing', and advised them to 'go and see the rest quickly'.*

London had, of course, been convulsed by bouts of rebuilding before. John Rennie Jnr, reflecting in his autobiography on the 1820s and 1830s, the period when he was engaged on London Bridge, recalled the capital being seized by 'a perfect mania for architectural improvements'. Then the Royal Mews had been levelled for Trafalgar Square. Hay carts curtailed on the Haymarket. Cross's Menagerie evicted from the Strand. And Nash's Regent Street, a prophylactic sheathing Mayfair from Soho in Portland

---

* Fletcher himself took a dim view of the Bridge House Committee's plans and the public's reaction to them. 'Few things,' he wrote in *London's River*, 'I think, could be more characteristic of the apathy of modern Londoners than their failure to protest against the proposal to demolish London Bridge and to replace it by a pre-stressed concrete affair equal in nastiness to Waterloo Bridge. Hardly a protest was made as far as I could make out: no demands to know why the settlement couldn't be corrected by underpinning or, if not, why a replica could not be built – nothing but mute acceptance.'

stone, unfurled as the axis for the West End. But 'the mania for architectural improvements' which was now intent on sweeping aside London Bridge was of an altogether different magnitude.

Its roots, naturally enough, lay in the post-war plans of the 1940s. During the Blitz, London *had taken it* – the city lost over 3.5 million homes – but on the tacit understanding that once the Luftwaffe's poundings were over, the resulting mess and whatever fetid, rat-infested back-to-backs had survived would be tidied away afterwards. In place of grime, muddle and pollution, a cleaner, greener, less crowded and more orderly metropolis was promised. Or at least alluded to, as a mote of ash was wiped from the teary eye of a stranger on the concourse of Victoria Station, say.

Tortured by images of shoeless children playing with lumps of coal on filthy doorsteps, planners like Patrick Abercrombie, who drafted the Greater London Plan with William Holford in 1944, proposed separating housing from industry. In turn, urban sprawl would be contained by the establishment of a green belt, a lung for London of fallow outlying land. Inner-city overcrowding and housing shortages would be eased with the creation of new towns with new industrial estates beyond it, in a planet-and-moon formation. Work on the first, Stevenage, was underway by 1946. These were to be supported by a series of new radial motorways and central ring roads with pedestrians catered for on road-spanning walkways – or pedways. Slums, meanwhile, would be cleared and superseded by modern homes fit for a modern London.

That was the plan, anyway.

In the event, with the country only kept from bankruptcy by the Marshall fund from America in 1947, rebuilding in London in particular progressed sketchily, with expediency besting intrepid remodelling for the most part. But then came the Festival of Britain in 1951. Although scaled back by Stafford Cripps' austerity measures, the festival, a trade and cultural jamboree in the spirit of the Great Exhibition sold to Attlee's Labour government by *News Chronicle* editor Gerald Barry shortly after the war, at last presented architects, planners, engineers and designers with a chance to show off their forward-thinking mettle in the capital. With the Skylon, a vertical steel sculpture that might easily have appeared in a Dan Dare space adventure in the *Eagle* comic, as its thrusting totem, a derelict patch of the South Bank became home to what the architect and writer Lionel Brett saluted as 'the long-awaited opening of the flower of modern architecture' in England. With the concrete, glass and asbestos of the Royal Festival Hall jostling for attention with displays of tweeds, models of characters from *Alice in Wonderland* and a replica English seaside resort, much of that modernity was pretty tame and undercut with whimsy – or overwhelmed by it, harsher critics argued. But in the not unreasonable opinion of its director of architecture Hugh Casson, 'it made people want things to be better and to believe they could be'. Even the initially sceptical Harold Nicolson confessed returning 'to the drab outside encouraged and entranced' by its vision of 'the New Britain . . . that is to be'.

But as austerity faded and affluence rose, attitudes hardened, expectations grew and the willingness to compromise shrank. With nearly full employment, and after the years of shortages, consumers with spare cash in their pockets were fed up with hand-me-downs, and weren't going to forgo any of the latest mod cons this New Elizabethan Age had to offer.

Thanks to the rebuilding of Coventry, architects too had seen what miracles could be performed with a free hand, a clean slate, some cash and a dollop of concrete, and were anxious to get on with the real business of converting Britain to the true faith of Le Corbusier.

The architects and consumers, in a sense, fuelled each other. In 1956, Alison and Peter Smithson, the architects later behind the 'brutalist' Robin Hood Gardens Estate in Poplar, presented their gadget-tastic plastic House of the Future at the *Daily Mail*'s Ideal Home Show at Olympia. 'In the American magazines of the 1940s and 1950s,' Alison Smithson later stated, 'we could foresee the consumer-orientated society that would, through advertisements, change all our lives . . . World War II had acted as a great divide between ourselves and our grandparent architects, who built for the few . . . and for the genteel who shopped for rarely replaced objects.'

With Harold Macmillan, in the role of Churchill's housing minister in the early 1950s, throwing money at new homes and holding a 'bonfire of controls' that opened the door to a welter of speculative developments, the country was on course for a bright Never Had It So Good future – a Britain perked up by HP-funded fitted carpets, fridges and television sets, and beset by ring roads, paved shopping precincts, large-scale housing estates, car parks and office blocks. And in London in 1956, the latter were given an enormous impetus when the Conservative government relaxed controls dating from 1888 restricting the height of buildings in the capital to a hundred feet – the reach, supposedly, of a fireman's ladder. (Though the softness of the city's underlying clay was another commonly voiced justification for the ruling.) Skyscrapers, to use the now rather quaint terminology of this, the Jet Age, mushroomed immediately at Stag Place in Victoria, and in Knightsbridge, Notting Hill Gate, St Giles Circus, Holborn, Haymarket and at London Wall in the City. Their lofty heads were hard to avoid now that the Clean Air Act had also banished the atmospheric, if lethal, smog from the capital. Most unavoidable of all was the twenty-six-storey Shell Centre. Occupying seven acres and rising to 350 feet, Howard Robertson's hefty tribute to the Rockefeller Center in New York was to be one of the largest office blocks in Europe when it opened on the South Bank in 1962.

By then the capital boasted 114 million square feet of offices, an increase of fifty per cent on 1938. A government report on 'Offices in London', meanwhile, claimed that of 200,000 new jobs created in central London between 1951 and 1961, 150,000 were office jobs. They estimated that a further 125,000 to 150,000 white-collar posts were likely to be added over the next ten years. Since offices workers, perfectly illustrated (or stereotyped) at this juncture by Tony Hancock as the bowler-hatted drudge and aspirant artist in *The Rebel*, were then deemed more likely to travel into the city from digs in the outer boroughs or homes in the leafy suburbs, the question remained: how exactly were London's roads and rail networks to cope with this influx?*

As it was, the number of vehicles on Britain's roads was already becoming a matter of serious concern. Having reached five million in the early 1950s, the figure had doubled to over ten million by 1962. The problem was, of course, especially acute in London where the number of cars registered went from 480,300 to 802,600 over the same period. Heavy congestion had resulted in the first parking meters being installed in Mayfair and Oxford Street in 1958. London County Council unleashed a series of road improvements at Euston, Elephant and Castle and the Blackwall Tunnel, intended to ease 'traffic flow and conditions, to increase capacity and to reduce delays'. One-way systems were established on Gower Street and Tottenham Court Road, Hyde Park Corner and Park Lane, while the extension of Cromwell Road and the completion of the Chiswick Flyover, opened in 1959 by the buxom Hollywood star (and, alas, future car-crash victim) Jayne Mansfield, 'more than doubled traffic' on the Great West Road and Western Avenue.

---

* Ian Nairn, who had a pretty low opinion of anyone who worked but didn't live in the capital, felt the whole character of the City was being 'flushed out' by what he vilified as 'the alien tide that flows in across London Bridge at 8.55 a.m. every Monday to Friday'. The word 'commuter' is itself an 'alien' import, hailing from the 'commutation tickets' (i.e. season tickets) sold on American railways from the late nineteenth century onwards. And if the Missouri-born T. S. Eliot provided the most memorable image of office workers trudging over London Bridge in *The Waste Land*, it is W. H. Auden in 'September 1, 1939', a poem written about the outbreak of the Second World War from the safety of neutral New Jersey, who is credited with introducing the word to British readers.

Around the same time that the architect and author G. A. Jellicoe was positing the concept of Motopia – a new form of city, tailor-made for man and automobile and, seemingly, to be built on the north banks of the Thames near Staines – and Hammersmith acquired its flyover, Ernest Marples, the minister of transport, set up a working group headed by Sir Colin Buchanan 'to study the long-term development of roads and traffic in urban areas'. Buchanan's report, *Traffic in Towns*, was published in 1963 and bolstered the prevalent orthodoxy that London had to be altered to meet the projected levels of car use. Simply crunching the numbers, numbers that admittedly came skewed with plenty of assumptions about the inexhaustibility of fossil fuels and the inevi-tability of car ownership and usage, Buchanan argued that if only a third of those predicted to drive in the capital were to be accom-modated, then over 'half of the physical fabric of the inner city' would have to be demolished. A six-lane freeway for Oxford Street with 'decks' above the roads for shops and pedestrians was among his suggestions for getting the city up to scratch.

These ideas were two a penny in the 1950s and early 1960s, when politicians, county councillors, bureaucrats, architects and developers of nearly every persuasion and stripe seem to have been gripped by a peculiarly missionary zeal to 'move with the times'. Modernisation was their watchword. And London, to an extent justly, was seen by its overlords as a cartographical embarrassment, a festering mess of haphazardly twisting, aged streets and decrepit tenements only coars-ened by war damage and gaudy Victorian 'improvements'. Like Vidal

Sassoon happily scissoring away bird-nest hair with his five-point cut, or TV's Mr DIY Barry Bucknell demonstrating how to cover unsightly panelled doors and fireplaces with plywood, their fingers itched for geometry, clean lines and neat finishes.

From drinking instant Nescafé, a supposedly energy-saving means of obtaining an energy-enhancing drink, to wearing easy-to-launder but mineral-depleting drip-dry shirts, greater efficiency was trumpeted as an unimpeachable benefit of living in the latter half of the twentieth century. It was irrelevant that the coffee was undrinkable, or that the shirts made you sweat: progress was . . . well, *progressive* – and something that no one, in any case, had a cat in hell's chance of standing in front of. Soon lunch would be a pill and electricity 'too cheap to meter' thanks to your neigh-bourhood nuclear reactor. Better, or so the thinking went in many a corridor of power (or often, not unconnectedly, a Soho club), to embrace it wholeheartedly than to settle for half measures.

Across the pond, America, and Los Angeles especially – less a traditional city than an entire motorised region – had provided the template for automotive urban growth. Its tall buildings, express-ways and drive-ins, idealised in photographs, Hollywood movies and popular songs, presented an irresistible notion of unfettered mobility. And after all, in a car, with the windscreen framing your vision, any approaching landscape unfolds just like a movie as a continuous kinetic sequence of startling images.*

---

* Lest we forget, in Britain in the 1960s, self-service supermarkets, quickly a mundane factor of everyday life, represented a glamorously transatlantic

Planners, meanwhile, were in awe of Robert Moses' New York 'Construction Coordinator'. Credited with making 'Baron Haussmann look like a subcontractor', Moses ploughed a six-lane expressway through the heart of the Bronx and waved the demolition of Penn Station through with an indifference to public outrage aloof enough to border on the positively vindictive.

This urge to completely remake civic space, and ideally violently, was incredibly seductive. 'Ask any self-respecting planner of 1963 how to renew London's outworn fabric', architect Peter Hall observed in his forward-looking manifesto *London 2000*, 'and the answer would come straight back: bring in the bulldozers. Rebuild from the ground up.' And such thinking swirled around one of the most contentious and long-lasting plans of the period; a proposal to construct a 'Motorway Box' in the capital. A revival in essence of Abercrombie's circular road scheme, but constructed in totality, it would have eviscerated large parts of Hackney, Camden, Hampstead, Shepherd's Bush, Fulham, Battersea, Lewisham and Greenwich, resulted in about 400 miles of motorway, cost £2 billion, and involved evicting some 100,000 people. In retrospect it appears unconscionable. But for nearly a decade the scheme was judged close to incontrovertible. With Barbara Castle, the transport minister in Harold Wilson's 1966 Labour administration, promising to democratise car ownership and spend

---

advancement. In the 1965 film of Len Deighton's spy thriller *The Ipcress File*, Colonel Ross, played with exquisite condescending superiority by the New Zealander Guy Doleman, tracks down his cockney upstart operative Harry Palmer, Michael Caine at his dapper best in horn-rimmed specs and knitted tie, in a supermarket and drolly confesses to not holding with these 'new American shopping methods'.

more money on roads, London and the South-East's whole prosperity was believed to hinge on its execution.*

In the end, the chill winds of the early 1970s' economic recession did as much to nip 'the Box' in the bud as a campaign by a growing band of articulate and self-interested middle-class property owners. Tellingly the sections of it that were completed, the Westway from Paddington to North Kensington and the East Cross Route from Hackney Wick to the Blackwall Tunnel, went through areas then characterised by deprivation. (And both areas were also beneficiaries of Erno Goldfinger tower blocks.)

In this rather intense climate, then, few landmarks were entirely free of the attentions of some bright spark with a drawing board, a notion or two about how they could be done away with, and the sympathetic ear of a County Hall official. And London Bridge was no exception.

For a flavour of opinion among the Corporation of London officials, easily summarised as 'out with the old, in with the new', an article from the January 1967 issue of their newsletter, *Guildhall*, is instructive. Writing about the construction of the Barbican estate, that perplexing-to-navigate wonder in Stickle Brick brutalism formed on the site of bombed-out Cripplegate, the piece argued that: 'The City has lived with its history for two thousand years, and in the process, the world too often seems to think that it has come to a

---

* Opening the Blackfriars Underpass in July 1967, Barbara Castle felt moved to compliment this four-lane roadway's 'modern attractive design', and saluted it as 'another step toward the unsnarling of London traffic'.

standstill, that it has become frozen in its past. This is not so . . . Today a new City is taking shape to meet the new and urgent needs of the third quarter of the twentieth century – a City of new build-ings and roads; of new pedestrian walkways and open spaces; of new schools, shops, theatres and concert halls. The City of London, in fact, is being reborn.'

And so, as if to further bolster the Corporation's neophiliac credentials, six months later the same paper would announce to the world that London Bridge, the cornerstone of that 2,000-year history, was up for sale.

The reasons given for London Bridge's death sentence were as predictable for the era as a Beatles number one.* 'The present bridge', explained the City Engineer Harold King, 'is inadequate to meet existing traffic needs.' At each of the rush-hour periods – and in an age when working days were more often than not still rigidly delineated by clocking in and clocking out, these passed in sharper, tidal peaks and troughs – it was calculated that 2,500 vehicles and 20,000 pedestrians were crossing the bridge. Barely altered since it was widened to sixty-five feet in 1902, London Bridge was an Edwardian gent valiantly trying to cope with the mores of the 1960s. In essence it was a pontine version of BBC TV's cryogenically preserved adventurer of the era, Adam Adamant.

The heaviest thing in London in 1831, its 130,000-ton carriageway

---

* Okay, perhaps not the best analogy in 1967, when Engelbert Humperdinck's 'Release Me' kept the Fab Four's 'Strawberry Fields Forever' and 'Penny Lane' single off the top spot but . . . even so.

was by the 1960s measured to be sinking at a rate of an eighth of an inch a year. The arrival of bulkier vans and lorries – with drivers gunning their Gardner engines while daydreaming of a mug of sugary tea and the waitress at the Blue Boar services – were only exacerbating its descent into the clay.

Its successor, touted as a bridge 'to meet the needs of a modern London', was, it emerged, to be a structure of three spans of pre-stressed concrete 105 feet wide – a forty-foot advance on the old bridge, which meant that the carriageways on each side could be beefed up from two to three lanes. Pedestrians, meanwhile, could look forward to striding along two walkways paved with York stone, one fifteen feet wide on the upstream and another of twenty-one feet on the downstream side. That lopsidedness was necessary to compensate for an unavoidable predilection for the downstream path among railway commuters. Filing out of London Bridge Station of a morning, any lingering tingle of Gibbs SR toothpaste completely obliterated by bacon, eggs and the third cigarette of the day, this army in pinstripes and twinsets marched north as one on to the nearest, right-hand lane to the City. Repeating the exercise at 5 p.m., thoughts perhaps turning to a pre-supper Tio Pepe, they magnetically gravitated south and left, hastening to reach their evening trains home.

The design was contrived to allow for the addition of a fully enclosed overhead walkway, if it should be required at a later date. In the original plans, pedestrians were also to be inhibited from stepping on to the carriageway by glazed barriers, whose other function was to offer protection from splashing as Routemaster buses and Ford Anglias tore through the puddles that, inevitably, would still form on its curved-towards-the-drains mastic asphalt surface. To help prevent icing in the winter months, however, both the carriageways and the pedestrian walkways were to be equipped with an innovative 'underfloor' heating system.

Although the new London Bridge appeared to have three arches, it would not technically be an arched bridge. Where the five arches of the Rennie bridge, like the nineteen of de Colechurch's before it, did the muscular business of holding the whole crossing up, the curves on its replacement were practically falsies, supplying only cosmetic support. The new bridge was to be fashioned, much like a motorway flyover, from 'four parallel pre-stressed concrete box beams – each', as Harold King pointed out, 'itself a complete bridge'.

The outer parapet of the bridge was to be encased 'in polished grey granite and surmounted by a stainless steel handrail', while the 'high strength concrete superstructure' was to be 'made with granite aggregate and then lightly etched by grit blasting to provide a plain grey concrete finish'. There are possibly fewer phrases less edifying today than 'plain grey concrete finish'. But within the context of the mid-to-late 1960s and a little beyond, such detailing remained aesthetically emblematic of high-minded and chic, go-getting civic projects.

Following the passing of the London Bridge Act in 1967, the contract for the new bridge was awarded to the trusted firm of consulting engineers Mott, Hay and Anderson, with John Mowlem and Co. tasked with its actual construction. An earlier incarnation of Mott, Hay and Anderson had first been employed by the Corporation of London to oversee the reconstruction of Rennie's Southwark Bridge in 1909. And throughout the 1950s they had made good the bomb scars of that structure and Tower Bridge and were subsequently engaged on numerous other projects in the capital, among them building a new river wall at Blackfriars.

What was described as 'the architectural treatment of the new bridge', meanwhile, came from William Holford and Partners, who were retained for the duration of its construction.

During the 1940s, William Holford had worked under Abercrombie on all the major post-war planning documents, until 1942 overseen in turn by Lord Reith, the severe first director general of the BBC. And although his tenure at the helm was relatively brief, most of the post-war rebuilding schemes did ultimately have a strongly Reithian flavour. Both Abercrombie and Holford were alumni of the Liverpool

University School of Architecture, though of differing generations. Abercrombie had become its professor of architecture in 1915 when his friend Edwin Lutyens, the architect famed for his eclectic neo-traditional country houses, remained quite the latest thing. Holford, born in Johannesburg in 1907, was a twenty-year-old undergraduate when Frederick Etchells' translation of Le Corbusier's *Vers une Architecture* – modern architecture's *Little Red Book* – was published. Most British architects before the Great War expected to earn their reputation, and a decent crust, on rural piles, banks, town halls and the odd church. But Holford and his student contemporaries, if still fed a dose of Beaux Arts beside the Mersey, were of an age to be excited by the prospect of skyscrapers, department stores and power stations. Historicism, if not bunk, was now slightly suspect, since the noble ideals underpinning it had only led to the slaughter in the trenches of the preceding generation. A better world would have to be built from scratch, or so much of the thinking behind a pervasive strand of modernism went. Though only up to a point; there were as many shades of modernism as neoclassicism, after all.

Holford was a complex man. Intellectually serious with aston-ishing powers of concentration, he was somewhat reserved, occa-sionally sour and professionally clinical. But he disliked 'airs' and could be funny, charming, and was judged handsome, not to say debonair. A photograph from the late 1930s has him wearing a rakish broad-brimmed fedora and what could possibly be a pair of the black suede brogues promoted to fashion by 'Mr Chatterbox' in Evelyn Waugh's *Vile Bodies*. Later in life – and signalling a determination not to be cowed by circumstance and a smidgen of vanity – rather than submit to glasses, Holford devoted himself to the Bates method for improving eyesight famously championed by Aldous Huxley. A left-leaning believer in socially improving, civic-minded architecture, many of his, and his wife's, closest friends in the capital were émigrés who had fled fascism.

Holford's own conversion to the modernist cause, or evidently a sense that the past was squatting like an odious hobgoblin on the present, occurred in Rome. Sent there on a scholarship to the British School in 1930, he found the city positively necrotising. 'Modern Rome', he maintained in a letter to his more radical college friend George Stephenson, 'is a thousand times more dead than ancient Rome. The ruins are altogether too powerful. They are the attraction and the destruction, the lure and the disadvantage of the city.' And when he submitted an essay for the 1932 RIBA competition, based on observations of southern Italy, Holford turned his guns on the baroque. Attacking its 'refinements' in modernist terms, he called for the 'gaily posturing remnants of the Great Baroque Masquerade' to be cleared 'as soon as possible' to leave disencumbered piazzas.

This urge to be free of the gaudier trappings of yesteryear would stand him in good stead as an architect and a town planner after the war, when he produced 'The Redevelopment of Central Areas', a document which became the 1947 bible for urban regeneration.

But in London, Holford was responsible for one of the worst planning disasters of the post-war period; a redevelopment many considered as much of an affront, an atrocity even, to the cityscape as the Blitz itself. Another of his schemes, one that had the potential to be far more devastating, hung in the balance for years before finally being kyboshed in the early 1970s.

The first was Paternoster Square at St Paul's. A year after its completion in 1967, viewers of the science-fiction TV series *Dr Who* were treated to the sight of the Cybermen, those jug-handle-headed metal men from Planet 14, marching down St Peter's Steps beneath the cathedral in an adventure self-explanatorily entitled 'The Invasion'. Fortunately for Earth, the eponymous Time Lord, neither of his two hearts skipping a beat, was easily able to defeat the icily mechanical fiends with a twiddle of his bow tie, a blast on his recorder, and a quick shimmy through a disused lift-shaft. The story, boasting a malevolent electronics industry magnate and an obdurate computerised receptionist, is a litmus test for late 1960s' anxieties about the dehumanising aspects of technology – of which the Cybermen themselves, as former humanoids grown ever crueller since they first began pawing the cutlery drawer with intent, are perfect examples.

The choice of location was itself far from arbitrary. For any adults watching this show, broadcast less than twenty-five years after the Second World War, the image of alien invaders menacing Wren's masterpiece would have had an added and unavoidable poignancy. The Great Dome's survival throughout the Blitz, nothing short of a miracle in the light of the incendiaries falling all about it, had resulted in the cathedral becoming a powerful symbol of Britain's indomitable wartime spirit. And yet anyone walking around Holford's new Paternoster Square, a deathly, wind-swept expanse of concrete, walled in by rows of unyieldingly monotonous blocks, could be forgiven for assuming that the Cybermen, if not actually the Nazis, had been victorious.

The City Corporation had appointed Holford to draw up plans for a worthy new setting for the cathedral in 1955, following the clearance of the bombed mess around it – what Graham Greene had memorably summed up as 'the obliterated acres of Paternoster Row' in his Blitz-era novel *The Ministry of Fear*. Holford envisaged integrating the church into the City with an arrangement of new office buildings and creating a traffic-free piazza, or 'a pool into which life would flow', as he once rather more fancifully phrased it, in front of the main entrance. And to be fair to Holford, whatever his original ideas were, he was soon assailed by a plethora of often conflicting demands from the Corporation, the London County Council and Duncan Sandys, the minister for housing and local government. Sandys, in particular, took a lively interest in the redevelopment and had a large-scale model of St Paul's set up in his office. There, and aided by piles of wooden blocks, he and Holford spent hour upon hour plotting and counter-plotting each possible scheme like a couple of war gamers re-fighting the Battle of Talavera with tin soldiers. Sandys, something of a technophile when it came to missiles, rockets and Polaroid cameras in his next position at the Ministry of Defence, was smitten with the whole notion of thrustingly up-to-date skyscrapers. Underwhelmed by one of Holford's early drafts, he wrote that the 'opportunity to provide some distinctive contribution to the skyline, by the construction of a tall building in the area to the north-west side of the Cathedral', was not to be missed.

Years ticked by, Sandys moved on to his new position, and several fresh plans were knocked out and other architects consulted, before a revised version of one of Holford's proposals was adopted in 1962. For all of the fingers in the pie, 'the conceptual weakness' of the development, nevertheless, lay fairly and squarely with Holford, and no sooner had the scaffolding gone up than the hideousness of what was to follow became painfully apparent. The dean of St Paul's, the Very Reverend W. R. Matthews, publicly called for an immediate halt to the work and it was denounced in the *Daily Telegraph* as a 'shameless and vulgar national scandal'. On 25 March 1964, a large demonstration against it was held at the site but to no avail.

Railing against the 'slabs of concrete' erected in the City between the end of rationing and the break-up of the Beatles, Robert Finch, the lord mayor of London, selected Paternoster Square as a prime blunder of the era in a piece for The *Guardian* in 2004. By then Holford's square had been redeveloped out of existence, but Old Paternoster, Finch recalled – and we can surely hear the gold chain chinking as he shuddered at the memory of it – was 'ghastly, monolithic . . . without definition or character'.

A criticism often levied during its lifespan of thirty-plus years was that even on warm, calm days, the square played host to a nippy breeze. This chilliness, while it endured, was, as a survey of Holford's output has noted, a persistent reminder of just 'how little was known in the mid-1950s about the effects of high buildings on the passage of air around them'.

So, we can be enormously grateful that Holford didn't get to have his way with that second great scheme of his: Piccadilly Circus.

Arguably enjoying a near-parallel existence in London during what could be called the rock'n'roll years to Times Square in New York, Piccadilly Circus continues to vie with Leicester and Trafalgar squares as 'the unofficial centre of the capital' – at least, as far as most tourists, seeking something, anything, tangible to photograph and orientate themselves by in the West End, are concerned. Laid out by Nash in 1819, the area was transformed into an ungainly vortex of converging streets in the 1880s when the Metropolitan Board of Works opted to plough their new Shaftesbury Avenue into the original 'circular' Regent Street and Piccadilly crossroad. Sir Alfred Gilbert, the artist tasked with creating its landmark 'Eros' statue, damned it as 'an impossible site . . . upon which to place any outcome of the human brain, except possibly an underground lavatory'. And it wasn't long before moralists had started to compare it to an open sewer. The electronically illuminated adverts for Bovril and Schweppes, handmaidens of mammon winking coquettishly at passers-by from buildings on the north-eastern perimeter as early as 1910, were vulgar enough. But Piccadilly Circus was already identified as a 'great centre for inverts' in 1905 by George Ives, the pioneering gay-rights campaigner and likely model for the fictional 'gentleman burglar' Raffles, who lives in bachelor chambers with his loyal manservant Bunny Manders in 'Albany' nearby. This was not to moralists' taste. The Lyons Corner House, roughly the Starbucks of its day and first established to the east of the Circus on Coventry Street in 1909, was affectionately known as the Lilypond by the men who cruised its upper-floor restaurant in the late evenings and at weekends into the 1950s. The News Theatre cinema, frequented by *Carry On* star Kenneth Williams, and the Underground Station, where Sir George Mowbray, president of Reading University Council, was arrested in 1946 for 'importuning men for an immoral purpose', were among the other local rendezvous favoured by homosexuals.* By the 1960s, 'the Dilly', predominantly thanks to the combined presence of an all-night Boots the Chemist and Dr

---

* An entry in Williams' diary for 20 June 1957, runs: 'Popped into the news theatre in Piccadilly! – phew! the gylrig going on!' The drift into the gay argot Polari speaks for itself really.

John Petro, a bankrupt medic who flogged prescription scripts at £3 a pop outside it, also became a Mecca for junkies.

Almost from the start, repeated attempts had been made to knock the Circus into a more respectable shape – morally and physically. But it wasn't until Jack Cotton, the wily Birmingham property speculator, purchased the bomb-damaged Café Monico building on the northern corner of Piccadilly Circus and Shaftesbury Avenue from Express Dairies in 1952 that plans for the wholesale redevelopment of the area began to take wind.

The London County Council were then champing at the bit to expand the roads and build a new roundabout to cope with the widely anticipated, and already perceptible, hike in car owner-ship, but were without the requisite funds from government to pull it off. Cotton wanted to squeeze as much as possible out of his investment, with the result that a series of increasingly cynical deals were struck between the two parties. Everything was going swimmingly until an ebullient Cotton got carried away and went public with his plans for the site in 1959. The central feature of the design was a *2001: A Space Odyssey*-style monolith of a building adorned with a hundred-foot high advertising hoarding. In the speculative drawings, this was dressed with a mock-up advert for an imaginary soft drink, with the fake slogan 'Snap Plom for Vigour' appearing in gigantic letters above the Circus. One commentator's overriding impression was that it looked like 'an enormous fruit machine' – and as such it provided critics in

Fleet Street with an off-the-shelf metaphor for the state of planning policy in London.

Questions were asked in the Houses of Parliament, a public inquiry was convened (chaired, incidentally, by Sir Colin 'Traffic in Towns' Buchanan), Cotton's plan halted, and drawing boards were returned to, with Holford awarded the job of coming up with something more 'civic'. What he unveiled in 1961 was acclaimed as 'a quite brilliant tentative scheme for the development of the area' by *Architects' Journal*. But over half a century on, anything approaching brilliance is harder to fathom.

Piccadilly Circus, in Holford's reimagining, would have consisted of 'a raised island piazza' standing some seven feet above roaring traffic on a new roadway. Eros was to be repositioned on top of a florist's shop erected on the Regent Street corner of this expanse of concrete. Covered decks would have escorted pedestrians over the traffic to and from the central piazza, while a set of escalators were to have led them down to an underground shopping concourse. Sundry tall office blocks, albeit with one co-designed by Walter Gropius, and a swanky new entertainment complex to be mounted on a platform, a replacement for the London Pavilion, were also in the mix. But Holford was to keep stirring this mix around a little too long, until, in 1967, the new Greater London Council, seeking a larger capacity for traffic in the wake of Buchanan's report, put his various drafts to one side, and sought fresh schemes from elsewhere. David Bowie's *Ziggy Stardust*, the album's cover image shot in a back alley off Piccadilly, would be in the top ten before the entire redevelopment was abandoned five years later.*

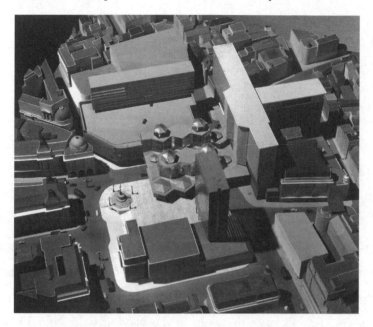

In the interim period, Holford and his partners at least had the satisfaction of watching their efforts taking shape elsewhere in the capital. On 6 November 1967 work commenced on the new London Bridge. But soon enough all the public would be interested in was the old one. Quite unexpectedly, it emerged that this pile of supposedly clapped-out stone was to be put up for sale. Would anyone really buy it, though? Ivan Luckin, a member of the Bridge House Estates Committee, was praying that they would.

---

* Its blueprints conceivably consigned to one of those overflowing rubbish bins outside K. West on Heddon Street that the Starman rests his eighteen-hole booted foot upon.

CHAPTER 7

The Man Who Sold the World a Bridge

Denis Thatcher knew him as Frankie. Frank, shorn of its bluntness, and a less saintly Francis, it is a name for boxers, gangsters, comics and crooners – and good-time dames. It's a singsong name that sounds like a toast, glasses of un-iced drinks (who'd want to dilute the alcohol?) chinked in the golf-club bar as conversation turns to pinkos at the BBC. It's a name more often conferred than chosen. And up there with Dickie, Willy, Freddie, Banksy, Milly, Bunty and Ginny, say, as a name first earned at public school. In Ivan Francis Luckin's case, that was on the playing fields of Mill Hill – his, and Denis Thatcher's, North London alma mater. But then the name is less important than the knowing. For Luckin – Ivan in the City, Frankie to Old Millhillians – made it his business to know people.

A champion cross-country runner in his late teens, he understood about persistence, distance and pacing: when to hold back, when to push in, and on. As a keen cub reporter on the *Morning Post* in the 1930s and then as City correspondent for the *Daily Telegraph*, he excelled at cultivating contacts to obtain the best stories. And Ivan loved a good story. But hankering to shape the news as much as report on it, he was drawn to public relations, a field still very much in its infancy in the UK. After the war, spent with the RAF Volunteer Reserve as a radar operator, and a stint on *Advertising Weekly*, he was hired in the 1950s to represent the New York-based publisher Fairchild and chaired the Publicity Club of London.

A bachelor, whose professional life, unfettered by family commitments, seems to have consisted of a never-ending cavalcade of press lunches, formal dinners, trade junkets and transatlantic business trips, Luckin was on the road to sixty before he threw himself into City of London Corporation politics. Elected to Candlewick Ward, one of the Corporation's ancient twenty-five wards of local government, in December 1964, he took the rather fateful step of joining the Bridge House Estates Committee, the body responsible for all the City's bridges, the following year. This was just as the motion to replace London Bridge with a new structure, held at amber for some months while Mott, Hay and Anderson drained flow charts of ink demonstrating to the Corporation that widening it again wasn't really viable, flicked to green.

Luckin liked the preliminary sketches of the blade of plain grey concrete destined to slice, or at least chisel, across the Thames in the old span's stead. But while discussions of the various merits of a pre-cast, post-tensioned concrete structure droned on, Luckin kept thinking more and more about the old bridge.

As a new boy on the committee, however, his questions about its fate were indulged with a polite, if never less than thinly veiled, contempt. The chair, C. F. Lewis, and City Engineer Harold King, initially bemused, soon found his curiosity irksome, judging it almost morbidly perverse. Their job was to improve the city and they quickly chalked up Luckin as one of those backward-looking stick-in-the-muds who believed London was never the same since the tearing down of the Maypole on the Strand in 1713. Their attitude baffled Luckin. He couldn't understand why anyone else hadn't spotted the gigantic bridge-shaped opportunity staring them in the face.

He'd broached the subject, cautiously, casually enough, at one of these early meetings, trying, if anything, not to appear overly excited by the brilliance of his own idea. 'Why not sell Old London Bridge?' That was all he'd said at first, as much later he grew rather fond of telling neighbouring diners at Corporation functions whenever other conversation lagged. The words had hung in the air for a few seconds before being batted away like sour cigarette smoke. But Luckin had persisted, raising it more formally in subsequent committee sessions. This could be the sale of the century, he argued. This was London Bridge – not some grubby Southwark-borders brick railway arch. *The* London Bridge. The genuine article. The response couldn't have been more negative. Asked how much he thought he would get for the old bridge, Luckin had answered, in all honesty, 'Not less than £1 million.' To which the committee's deputy chair, Donald Erlebach, doing nothing to hide his incredulity, had shot back, 'Mr Luckin, do you *really* believe anyone would pay that sum for a heap of stones?'

Luckin did. And from the very beginning, he maintained that the most likely purchaser was to be sought in America. He based this assumption on a good deal of precedence, rather than the stereotype, common enough in England at the time, that most Yanks had more money than sense. Though the person this former Fleet Street hand most admired for setting much of that precedent, William Randolph Hearst, arguably had more money than was sensible for a while. But today the insanity of what this newspaper titan spent – or wasted, less charitable souls might say – his fortune on looks positively admirable. At least when placed beside the dreary outlays of modern American stock-option-counting billionaires. One has to look to Elvis Presley or Michael Jackson for anything comparable.

A large, if softly spoken man, fluent in French and German, and inclined to loud hand-painted ties and brightly coloured suits, Hearst has been all but eclipsed by his cinematic representation – Orson Welles' immortal caricature, Charles Foster Kane. But the truth, already partially fictionalised by Aldous Huxley in his 1939 novel *After Many a Summer*, was odd enough without the shattered snow globes and seamless through-the-nightclub-roof tracking shots.*

A decade before *Citizen Kane*'s release, P. G. Wodehouse was a guest at Hearst's own Xanadu, San Simeon in California –

---

* In July 1939 Huxley, newly installed in California, celebrated the completion of the book by attending a Hollywood party where he met Orson Welles for the first time – Welles had only just signed a contract with RKO pictures. He was full of bluster about his plans to direct a film version of Joseph Conrad's *Heart of Darkness*, while Huxley let it be known that he'd written a novel featuring a character based on Hearst. A year after this encounter, Welles, having seemingly put the Conrad adaption on the back burner, began shooting *Citizen Kane* for RKO.

a Mediterranean-style palace of 165 rooms its owner called, with epic understatement, 'my little hideaway'. The creator of Jeeves and Wooster, who noted, in astonishment, 'Hearst collects everything', left a memorable description of the magnate's treasure-stuffed abode in its prime.

> The ranch [Wodehouse wrote in February 1931] is about halfway between Hollywood and San Francisco. It is on the top of a high hill, and just inside the entrance gates is a great pile of stones, which, if you ever put them together, would form an old abbey which Hearst bought in France and shipped over and didn't know what to do with so left lying by the wayside. The next thing you see, having driven past this, is a yak or a buffalo or something in the middle of the road. Hearst collects animals and has a zoo on the premises, and the ones considered reasonably harmless are allowed to roam at large. You're apt to meet a bear or two before you get to the house. The house is enormous, and there are always at least fifty guests staying there. All the furniture is period, and you probably sleep on a bed originally occupied by Napoleon or somebody.

As a ten-year-old, Hearst had accompanied his mother, Phoebe, a former schoolteacher, on an epic eighteen-month tour of Europe – the pair visiting every significant museum, gallery, ruin, castle and church in Ireland, Scotland, England, France, Italy, Switzerland,

Austria, Germany, Belgium and Holland, and dining with American consuls, and meeting the Pope in Rome, along the way. And it's impossible not to see much of Hearst's adult life as an elaborate attempt to recreate, physically, piece by piece, the highlights of that tour from a jumble of consoling prepubescent memories. Winston Churchill, another Hearst house guest, summed him up as 'a grave simple child – with no doubt a nasty temper – playing with the most costly toys'.

An omnivorous sweeper-up of old stuff, Hearst would buy the complete contents – tiled floors to chandeliers and everything in between – of French chateaux, Venetian palazzos and English country houses and have them reassembled in his various American mansions. The collecting more than outstripped the reassembling, with the result that countless old masters, carved ceilings and classical statues languished in a five-storey warehouse in the Bronx that Hearst soon filled with his surplus purchases. As Wodehouse's account confirms, whole buildings were far from immune from his attentions either. In 1925 alone, Hearst bought a twelfth-century Spanish Cistercian monastery, Santa Maria de Ovila, and St Donat's, an eleventh-century Welsh castle. The monastery, emulating the journeys of its compatriot conquistadors, was shipped west to California. The castle, which he had first spied in the pages of *Country Life*, was left *in situ* fourteen miles outside Cardiff. But finding its 130-odd rooms 'small dark and airless', after a single evening's stay, Hearst had its interiors completely gutted and a tennis court and swimming pool installed in the grounds.

One of Hearst's heroes was the nineteenth-century French architectural reformer Eugène-Emmanuel Viollet-le-Duc. Viollet-
le-Duc was France's great champion of Gothic architecture and
he restored many of the country's medieval cathedrals, most
famously Notre-Dame, and the fortress at Carcassonne. But he
viewed restoration as a creative art, pointedly adding an additional
flèche (spire) here and a gargoyle salvaged from somewhere else
there, with the intention of making each building look 'more'
Gothic than the original Gothic. Hearst admired this approach,
and brought comparably wonky levels of historical verisimilitude
to his own properties.

For instance, at St Donat's Hearst felt that outbuildings of the
type in movies that are never safe from torch-wielding emissaries
of 'Bad' King John would enhance the general ambience of the
castle. So he bought a medieval tithe barn and other remains from
Bradenstoke Priory in Wiltshire. He had these taken down timber
by timber and stone by stone, boxed up and transported to Wales.
These were later dismantled again and sent to San Simeon, where
they remained unpacked in crates until 1960 – nine years after
Hearst's death – when they were sold to the proprietor of the
Madonna Inn in San Luis Obispo. But their initial removal from
Wiltshire had caused the Society for the Protection of Ancient
Buildings (SPAB), who just a few years later would fight unsuc-
cessfully to save John Rennie's Waterloo Bridge from demolition

by the London County Council,* to post notices in London Tube stations alerting the public to Hearst's activities. Their campaign against Hearst resulted in questions being asked in the House of Commons. Sir Charles Allom, knighted for his restoration of Buckingham Palace and employed by Hearst on St Donat's, rallied to the American's defence, arguing that the tycoon was saving buildings that otherwise would fall to rack and ruin.

The fear, widespread in the interwar years, that Europe's cultural treasures were gradually being spirited across the Atlantic wasn't without foundation – nor solely down to Hearst. In 1909, and with lasting significance for Luckin and London Bridge nearly sixty years on, the American government adopted the Payne–Aldrich Tariff. This piece of legislation exempted objects more than a century old and considered works of art from import duties. The immediate effect of the bill was fairly muted, as far as antiques went. But following the First World War, when many a count or contessa was left with more wall hangings than cash, and more heirlooms than earnings, and sovereign nations needed

---

* This fight was spiced with an ideological dimension, pitting as it did the Labour leader of the LCC, Herbert Morrison, against both the SPAB (which had originally been founded by the socialist Pre-Raphaelite artist William Morris back in 1877) and what Morrison viewed as the reactionary forces of the establishment: Stanley Baldwin's Conservative government and Lord Rothermere's right-wing press. Morrison, whose flair for publicity, if perhaps not his politics, Ivan Luckin would have admired, eventually demonstrated the LCC's authority on 21 June 1934, when he ceremonially wielded a sledgehammer to knock out the first stone in the demolition of the bridge. A speedily published souvenir pamphlet entitled *Waterloo Bridge: Its Swan Song*, concluded that 'posterity, if not all today, will thank Herbert Morrison abundantly for having the courage to face facts'.

funds to rebuild, the trade in European artefacts grew brisk until dampened by the Depression, whose casualties in the end included Hearst.

But one of the after-effects of the Second World War, and the arrival of the Cold War, was a more general increase in transcontinental traffic among people and artworks.

America had, of course, largely bankrolled the rebuilding of Europe after the war and its tourist dollars were no less necessary, however begrudgingly pocketed, to Continental travel agents, hoteliers, restaurants, art galleries, museums and gift shops in the 1950s and 1960s. There was also a political school of thought in the States, as Christopher Endy notes in his book *Cold War Holidays*, that held that visiting Americans presented Europeans with a symbol of freedom and prosperity, one that the Soviets, relying on touring deputations of Olympic shot-putters and busy erecting concrete 'iron curtains' in their midst, were unable to counter.

In any case, many American ex-servicemen had spent parts of the conflict on the Continent, and had sentimental reasons for wishing to revisit countries they'd helped liberate. And the jet age, ushered in by the maiden flight of the De Havilland Comet in 1952, now made Paris, Rome or London far less remote and much more affordable destinations to visit for an increasingly affluent country. As Tom Wolfe has commented, 'the reason American tourists became a byword for vulgarity in Europe was that suddenly there were working-class Americans going abroad. There was never such a

LONDON BRIDGE IN AMERICA

period before . . . astonishing amounts of money had come into ordinary people's homes.'

What did these American come to see? The sights, naturally. For London that was Westminster Abbey, the tower of Big Ben. And if country singer Roger Miller's 1966 hit 'England Swings', a US Billboard chart topper, was to be believed, also children whose cheeks were rosy, gentlemen dapper in Derby (i.e. bowler) hats and policemen, without revolvers, bicycling in twos. This was the mythic, enduringly historic London, a city of toy castles, warm beer, cold baths, bad plumbing and worse food, where toasts to Dick Turpin, the clank of tankards and the rattle of pin-tables cheered every Soho pub. And its popularity – at least as an idea, foggy in popular imagining and in hard, verifiable detail – among Americans was what made Ivan Luckin certain that he'd find a stateside buyer in the vein of Hearst for London Bridge.

Luckin was fully aware – as others on the committee must have been – that while he was outlining his idea of a sale, over at Westminster College in Fulton, Missouri, where Winston Churchill had delivered his Sinews of Peace (i.e. 'Iron Curtain') speech in 1946, the ground was being broken in preparation for a stone-by-stone shipment of the remnants of London's St Mary Aldermanbury Church. This war-damaged Wren church was to be pieced back together and restored to its former glory in the Midwest as a memorial to Britain's late wartime leader – a leader whose coffin had been conveyed by barge along the Thames and under London Bridge as part of his state funeral in January 1965.

Luckin's real brainwave now was to argue that they could and should market *this particular* bridge as the embodiment of London's 2,000-year history. The committee had to forget all about John Rennie, his sons, and 1831. This was not any old lump of nineteenth-century granite hindering drivers of Ford Consuls from reaching their destinations, it was a lump of nineteenth-century granite that could trace its roots right back to the Roman conquest and which then ran right up to date with Churchill's funeral. And all that history would be worth something, possibly over £1 million, to somebody. It was just a question of finding that somebody with £1 million to spare.

There were, however, plenty on the committee who argued that all that history was exactly the kind of anachronistic baggage the City had to be seen dumping, and sharpish, if it was to have any future at all. Would, for instance, Luckin prefer it if they all came to meetings in togas? Or went bear-baiting, after the Livery dinners? And on it went, until the autumn of 1966, when at last Luckin mustered enough support for a special subcommittee to be formed to oversee the sale.

Springing into action, Luckin formulated an international publicity campaign and had a promotional brochure commissioned. Published on thick, quality paper, and richly illustrated throughout, this document outlined the precise technical details of the sale but was dominated by an evocative potted history of the bridge from AD 45 to the modern day. Heavy on marauding Norse invaders, saintly City fathers, traitors' severed heads on sticks, and John Rennie's engineering genius, it was a decidedly slick production, with prospective purchasers invited to submit closed bids on a facsimile of a nineteenth-century tender notice. There was little to indicate what would count as an acceptable bid, but then the card stock alone suggested that if you had to ask you probably couldn't afford it. Luckin had 2,000 of these brochures printed and distributed to every diplomatic outpost around the globe in July 1967.

An official press release mostly likely written by Luckin stated quite emphatically that the Corporation was 'determined not to sell the bridge piecemeal' and that it was 'not worthy for a great historic monument to be broken up and sold little by little'. This view marked a significant advance on official opinion of only five years earlier. Then, admirers of nineteenth-century architecture had been forced to look on in horror at various wanton acts of corporate vandalism.

Two of these stood out. The first was the Euston Arch. Erected in 1837 as the portico to the London & Birmingham Railway's new Euston Station, one of the first metropolitan train terminals in Europe, Philip Hardwick's Greek propylaeum – not technically an arch but a replica of the type of porch found on temples – was the largest ever constructed. Passing through it, the rail traveller was carried off in a puff of smoke, heady as incense, to arrive a little later and probably having ingested a rather desiccated cheese and pickle sandwich, in some distant realm: Tring, Llandudno or Runcorn. But in the light of the Conservative government's 1954 rail modernisation plan, 'the Arch' seemingly appeared as much of a dotty, anachronistic obstacle to British Transport Commission schemes for redeveloping Euston as the indefatigable Mrs Wilberforce in *The Ladykillers* was to the criminal ambitions of Professor Marcus and his eccentric gang. The British Transport Commission was determined to be rid of it. And while the free-wheeling Labour MP, journalist and TV presenter Woodrow Wyatt, the architectural historian and chair of the Victorian Society, Nikolaus Pevsner, Sir Charles Wheeler, the president of the Royal Academy, the poet John Betjeman and even the Brutalist architects Alison and Peter Smithson led a popular campaign to save Hardwick's masterpiece, it was to no avail. Although the contractor hired for the demolition, Frank Valori, had offered to number the stones so they could be stored and reassembled else-where, the bulk of the Euston Arch was finally dumped into the River Lea.

Just as preservationists were recovering from that body blow, in 1962 the Coal Exchange on Lower Thames Street, opened by Prince Albert in 1849, was felled in a prospective road-widening plan. Although the roadwork was not destined to start until 1972 and

the National Gallery of Victoria in Melbourne, Australia, had wanted to adopt the Exchange's unique cast-iron interior rotunda as the centrepiece of its new gallery, a Corporation of London official flatly informed its would-be saviours that the City could not 'spend time on the preservation of a Victorian building'. By the end of the year, it was gone, the iron picked over by scrap-metal merchants and most of its elegant glass smashed and ground down.*

By 1967, though, a corner had definitely been turned. St Pancras Station, much to the annoyance of the British Transport Commission, who could hardly wait to tear this monument to high Gothic architecture down, was listed thanks to the efforts of Sir John

---

* The film-maker Derek Jarman, looking back on his days as a student in London in the early 1960s, recalled that there 'was no love of Victoriana – Betjeman was a cosy voice on the *Third Programme*. None of us could have cared less as the Euston Arch fell . . . There was a hunger for the new – these old buildings seemed as dated as the class system which was still firmly in place.'

Betjeman, The Victorian Society and Nikolaus Pevsner. And in that same year, the Civic Amenities Act was passed giving local authorities the power to assign 'conservation' status to areas under their jurisdiction. And, strikingly, the sale of London Bridge itself was presented, and emotively, as an act of preservation. 'We could either destroy, totally, what is a piece of historic London,' the Corporation maintained, neatly sidestepping any other plausible alternatives, 'or try to sell it so that one of the world's most famous landmarks will be preserved for posterity.' The release concluded: 'We believe that the bridge could not only serve a useful function for it is still structurally quite sound, but also because we feel that London Bridge, which has served the city so well, deserves a decent future.' It was now just a question of waiting to see what, or where, that future might be.

CHAPTER 8

Sale of the Century

News that London Bridge was for sale first broke on 12 July 1967 – the day before the Corporation of London's Common Council were to take their final vote on the proposal. The vote was a mere formality but the advance appearance in the papers, indubitably Luckin's handiwork, suggests he wasn't leaving anything to chance. The *Guardian*, citing an unnamed Corporation spokesman, ran the story with the headline 'London Bridge may be up for sale' – the 'may be' an all important qualifier. Its reporter, John Fairhall, light-heartedly invoked an air of nefarious spivery about the proceedings. His opening line, 'Psst! Want to Buy London Bridge?', planted the reader firmly in the demi-monde of pencil-moustached sharpies, long camel-hair coats and fedora hats pulled low, with suitcases of black-market nylons and counterfeit Rolexes to offload. Though as Fairhall acknowledged, the Corporation did 'not intend to make a profit' from the sale and 'would charge a purchaser only the extra demolition costs involved in numbering up the pieces of masonry and fittings and taking them apart with sufficient care to permit rebuilding'. The buyer would also, he explained, have to cough up for the freight charges and the costs of putting the facade back together again at their end. Elaborating on the view that the

Corporation expected most interest to come from Commonwealth countries and America (the spokesman was keen to stress that offers from the latter would be regarded no less favourably), Fairhall contended that London, South Ontario, would provide the most suitable new home for London Bridge. 'The city', he wrote, 'even has a River Thames running through it, spanned by Westminster Bridge and Blackfriars among others. Its streets have some familiar names, such as Oxford Street and Piccadilly, and the Canadian Londoners can shop at their own Covent Garden Market.' Ten days later, by which time the sale had the Common Council's backing, the *Illustrated London News* stated that two Canadian cities, Winnipeg and Victoria, British Columbia, were 'said to be interested' in buying the bridge.

With curious synchronicity, the bridge's availability was announced at virtually the same moment as a deal was signed to sell the RMS *Queen Mary* to Long Beach, California. Once the Cunard–White Star line's flagship transatlantic liner and a gigantic three-funnelled, multi-decked sandwich wedge of a vessel, the *Queen Mary* had embarked on its maiden voyage to New York from Southampton in May 1936. Named after King George V's consort, Mary of Teck, it expressly catered to royals, celebrities, industrialists and presidents, and its high-end Anglo-American clientele were epitomised by the Duke and Duchess of Windsor, who were frequent passengers. The ship could practically have been constructed with their romance in mind. Its original interiors, a fogeyish spin on art deco fashioned in 'beautiful woods' from all corners of the empire and dismissed by Charles Ryder in *Brideshead Revisited* as if 'designed for a railway coach and preposterously magnified', quite deliberately aped the decor of gentlemen's clubs and country houses as they were portrayed in Hollywood movies. The aim was to satisfy rich American travellers' expectations of classic English upper-class style. Though refitted after service as a troop carrier during the war, it was to remain forever marooned in the leisurely, ocean-spanning age typified by quoits on the upper deck, co-respondent shoes, Artie Shaw and His Orchestra, dressing for dinner and copper-lettered invitations to the captain's table. Rendered obsolete by the arrival of mass-market jet-air travel in the 1960s, it was now sold to become a floating museum.

The potential loss of not one but two historic emblems of British engineering prowess caused more than a few murmurs of disquiet. John Jennings, the Conservative MP for Burton, would subsequently table a question to the government demanding to know whether they were willing to take any 'steps to prevent the sale of London Bridge to interests in a foreign country'. Niall MacDermot, responding for the ruling Labour administration, replied that since its demolition had been authorised by Parliament, he had 'no power to prevent the sale of its constituent parts, and he would not think it right to seek to do so'. The timing was, in a sense, unfortunate. Only the previous November, Harold Wilson had devalued the pound. An action taken in the hope of boosting exports to shore up the faltering manufacturing base, it was nevertheless widely portrayed as being as treasonous an insult to national prestige as putting the Queen on the game. For naysayers, totems of decline (metaphorical or otherwise) appeared all too readily to hand (with letters of the what-next-evict-the-ravens-from-the-Tower-*nihil-sanctum-est* variety a staple of the correspondence pages).

The story of the *Queen Mary*'s sale to Long Beach was also to take on a slightly unsavoury aspect. No sooner had Cunard publicised the deal than the manner in which the company had hawked the old girl was called into question. A syndicate from New York, headed up by Mr Huntington Hartford, the A&P stores heir, and the eccentric elderly multimillionairess Miss Rose Elkins, a resident of the Waldorf Astoria since the day it opened, who had entered a rival bid for the ship, launched a legal challenge to the deal. They claimed the shipping firm had not honoured the confidentiality of the auction. Their sealed postal bid, they maintained, had been leaked, allowing a delegation from Long Beach, who'd journeyed to London to present their offer to Cunard in person, a last-minute chance to up their digits. The matter was settled in Cunard's and Long Beach's favour.

With London Bridge, the Corporation of London, naturally, were anxious to avoid any similar hints of impropriety, and duly let it be known that the decorum of the bids would be judged as important as any amount of money offered.

By September, the Corporation was able to report a 'phenomenal' response with 'over a hundred requests for further information' coming from America, Canada, France, Switzerland and, on home turf, Devon and Sussex, bids already ranging from 'a deposit of one hundred dollars from a Virgin Island Consortium to an outright offer of £25,000 from a Rochester, Kent, man'. More apocryphal were an 'unconfirmed' story about a Texan who supposedly telephoned offering 'to top all bids' and the antics of a mysterious wealthy 'private collector' who after writing to arrange a viewing of the bridge failed to turn up for the appointment and never troubled the Corporation again.

As was probably to be expected, the majority of the letters they received were from cranks and souvenir hunters. This was, after all, a time when barely an evening's telly passed without Mary Whitehouse and her disgusted-of-Swizzlewick cohorts firing off green-inked missives to the BBC. But grasping the opportunity to generate some positive PR, and, of a kind destined to play well in Canada, the Corporation issued a press statement about one appealingly ingenuous letter from seven-year-old Roderick Todd in Victoria, British Columbia, that had arrived with a $2 bill tucked inside. 'Why', Roderick began, 'are you going to take London Bridge Down? My Mummy says that you are selling it. Can I buy some? Is this enough money for some?' Since this was, allegedly, the first request of this type they'd received, young Roderick was rewarded with a piece of bridge and his money back.

Potential bidders and requests, of one kind or another, continued to flood in, and Luckin offered to act as a roving ambassador, visiting interested parties and scouting out their proposed locations for the bridge. Unwilling to fund what some members, perhaps not unreasonably, saw as a round-the-world ticket to ride, the majority of the Common Council contended that, *à la* the *Queen Mary*, anyone serious about buying London Bridge would surely come to London. But to inject a greater sense of urgency, and kick serious offers into play, a closing date of 29 March 1968 was now established for bids.

By February, the Common Council still found itself without an acceptable, concrete, on-the-table offer for the bridge. Though there was over a month to go until the deadline, Luckin succeeded in persuading the Corporation to let him and Harold King, the City Engineer, travel to the United States to court further interest there. Doffing a cap to Paul Revere, Luckin hurriedly convened a press conference on the bridge to let the Americans know that the British were coming. Film footage of this event was swiftly flown out to New York and news of their forthcoming trip and the sale syndicated across the States.

But their visit was also the subject of a drolly humorous column in the *Observer* on 10 March by the American journalist John Crosby. Crosby related that Luckin and King were to 'interview eight American syndicates eager to buy London Bridge and put it up somewhere in America, not necessarily over a river'. With the *Queen Mary* in Long Beach being 'used for conventions, amusements, just about everything *except* transportation', he fully expected London Bridge to 'become a supermarket or a bordello'. The British, he argued, warming to the theme, had to be cautious about selling 'little bits of England', especially when his compatriots and real estate were concerned. Think back to Louisiana, he advised, or 'look at Alaska', or 'better still look at Howard Hughes'. The reclusive millionaire, Crosby maintained, had 'started buying one measly little hotel in Las Vegas' and now he had 'the airport and half the town' and probably wouldn't rest until he had 'all of Nevada'. These things, he pointed out, tend to get out of hand. 'This week it's London Bridge, next week Chelsea Bridge.' Before long, he warned, everyone would be 'swimming to Battersea'.

What Crosby didn't mention here (and why would he?) was his own minor, but not insignificant part, in bolstering London's standing – and the desirability of its real estate – among Americans. Once disparaged as 'the fellow who watches television for the *New York Herald Tribune*' by P. G. Wodehouse (who couldn't imagine a 'more appalling job'), Crosby, after moving in front of American TV cameras for a period in the late 1950s, came to Europe – to Paris first, and then London in 1964. Either as an act of gross ingratiation, unusual in a critic previously acclaimed for 'slaying with zest', or a heartfelt enthusiasm for what he found, Crosby wrote an article for the *Sunday Telegraph*'s colour supplement on 16 April 1965 entitled 'London – The Most Exciting City'. Here he played John the Baptist to *Time* magazine's better-known 1966 Christ, the famous 'Swinging London' issue, describing the capital 'as the swinging-est city'.

Perhaps the word 'swinging' today reeks a little too much of car keys tossed in punchbowls and wife-swapping in net-curtained semis in Ruislip. And Crosby, divorced from his first wife in 1959, wasn't above lasciviousness. 'Young English girls take to sex,' he wrote, practically salivating at the prospect, 'as if it's candy and it's delicious.' His vision of fashionable London, erring as it did (and naturally enough in the *Telegraph* back then) more towards upmarket clubland and the scions of the aristocracy than the mythical new popocracy of working-class hairdressers, beat musicians and photographers, was unquestionably geared to men of his age and inclinations: mostly wealthy, middle-aged, aspiring Frank Sinatras in snap-brimmed hats crooning 'A Nightingale Sang in Berkeley Square' in their cups in Shepherd's Market. But as a succinct precis of a place at that moment and a commodifiable idea of urbanity, real or partially imagined, his vision had enormous traction.

London had, of course, been quietly doing its 'own thing', to use the lingo of this dawning Age of Aquarius, without Crosby's help. Carnaby Street clothier John Stephen – who told Crosby, 'Buyers from American department stores come here and are absolutely astounded at what is happening. Why – they say – is this happening here and not in America?' – had been contentedly selling his 'Swiss fabric' sweater shirts to discerning gentlemen for nearly eight years. Further west, and in new larger art-nouveau-styled premises on Kensington High Street, Barbara Hulanicki had little difficulty pressing Biba dresses on the likes of Julie Christie. And on the top floor of 7 Leicester Place, in the mirror-lined Ad Lib club, the munching of chicken in a basket for a pound and the sipping of ten-shilling whisky and Cokes within gazing distance of go-go dancers, Jean Muir and a Beatle or two, continued unabated night after night. But Crosby's piece corralled all these disparate elements and others into 'a scene' where 'the action' was and gave it a name: 'Swinging London'.

Americans had, it should be stressed, always found Britain, or London, 'interesting' or more accurately, perhaps, 'quaint'. Previously England had been uptight, old, cold and grey, which wasn't without its appeal.

Even local bucks about town weren't averse to drawing un-favourable attention to these differing positions of the two nations: Peter Cook impersonating Harold Macmillan as a senile duffer meeting the 'young, vigorous' President Kennedy in 1961, say. But that impersonation helped carry Cook to Broadway and, along with the bowler-hatted clarinettist Acker Bilk's Billboard number one 'Stranger on the Shore', formed the advance guard of the so-called British Invasion that was to follow the Beatles' first visit to the States in February 1964. Now America was developing a taste for the British as 'uninhibited' and 'cool', in the sense of youthful, hip, happening, yeah baby yeah, lose that arm tiger.

And it wasn't just British youth culture that was suddenly in demand. One of the more intriguing developments in British pop, post Haley–Elvis-inspired rock'n'roll but pre loveable mop-top Beatles, was a brief vogue for old music-hall numbers and comic songs delivered in demotic London accents. Often these were performed by the same musicians who only a year or so earlier had been wailing about railroads down in New Orleans as if baptised in the Mississippi. For Lonnie Donegan and Tommy Steele the journeys from 'Cumberland Gap' and 'Rebel Rock' to 'My Old

Man's a Dustman' and 'What a Mouth' proved a short skip and a jump down Denmark Street on a road to becoming 'all-round' entertainers. But Mike Sarne's 'Come Outside' and 'Will I What?' and Bernard Cribbins' 'Hole in the Road' and 'Right Said Fred', the latter two produced by future Beatles knob-twiddler George Martin, were championed on release by George Melly for capturing the 'feel of the new working class with its non-forelock-tugging approach to the bourgeois and determination not to be kicked around'. Melly, heartened by their popularity, felt that 'on a modest scale' these records were 'the equivalent of the New Wave in British cinema'. If these particular discs, like some of the finer (and baser) indigenous movies of the era, were just a little too localised to 'travel', then Lionel Bart, one of Tommy Steele's main songwriters, and the singer–actor Anthony Newley took Manhattan by storm in 1962 with the cockney musicals *Oliver!* and *Stop the World – I Want to Get Off*.

These gutter-sparrow shows had struck a chord with American audiences.* Then came the appearance in *Vogue* of posh-but-didn't-look-stuffy Jean Shrimpton, snapped by another irrepressible little East End chappie, David Bailey, and finally topped off by the arrival of the Beatles themselves – four chirpy, working-class lads in *Twist*-like urchin caps, that admittedly probably owed

* For instance, the *New York Times*, evidently fearing another Jimmy Porter (and in that paper's review of Tony Richardson's American-financed film of *Look Back in Anger* in 1959, the character was denounced as 'a consistent weakling, a mature cry baby'), praised Newley for being 'young but not angry'.

more to Bob Dylan than Dickens. Their success, accompanied by the release of the first James Bond movies – and Sean Connery's Scottish vowels sounded British but meritocratically non-U to American ears – ushered in what the film critic Alexander Walker referred to as the 'Love Anything British' phenomenon. This Anglophilia was a phenomenon that would see the Beatles' American contemporaries, the Byrds, release their debut single under the cash-in name the Beefeaters, and Herman's Hermits achieve a stateside number one with the Edwardian music-hall standard 'I'm Henery the Eighth, I am'. Over in Hollywood, meanwhile, two musical pictures, *Mary Poppins* and *My Fair Lady*, with sound-stage belle époque London backdrops and peopled by h-dropping flower girls, imperious phonetics experts, unflappable nannies and dancing chimney sweeps, would clean up at the 1964 Oscars. *My Fair Lady* was awarded Best Picture and *Mary Poppins* went on to become the most profitable film of 1965.

A year later, and with even *Time* magazine's own 'Swinging London' issue by now mildewing amid discarded back numbers of *National Geographic* in dentists' waiting rooms, Anthony Newley, who as a child had appeared as the Artful Dodger in David Lean's 1948 film of *Oliver Twist*, was to appear in an hour-long Lucille Ball television special entitled *Lucy in London*. Here Newley chauffeurs the fifty-something American star around the 'Swinging-est City' in a motorcycle and sidecar combination. A typical exchange, ladling on the 'Yes, folks, Here We Are in Swinging London Town' exposition, runs:

NEWLEY: The King's Road, Chelsea, and Carnaby Street are the fashion centre of the London Mods.

BALL: Oh the Mods, I've heard about them, I am just crazy about their wild clothes.

And so on, as the pair trundle through a variety of comic and musical set pieces that pitch Ball's faux ditzy persona against an array of 'colourful' local characters, chisellers and jobsworths mostly, interspersed with performances by camp Shakespearean actors and finger-clicking choreographed dancers in op-art patterned dresses and striped waistcoats.

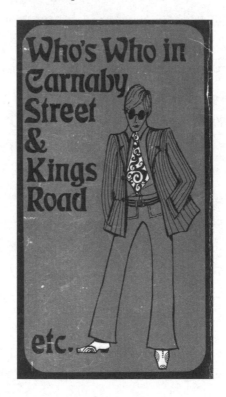

The show's closing theme song was written and, more unusually, sung by Wall of Sound producer Phil Spector. It provides a handy reductive, retrospective chronicle of the events portrayed but betrays a peculiar tin ear for the city's geography, name-checking the real Carnaby Street and the achingly hip Scotch of St James's alongside somewhere called 'Chelsea Street', while noting, with a nod to the nursery rhyme, the coming down of bridges and people dashing around. This is also a reference to another sequence in the programme, where Newley and Ball meet the Dave Clark Five on the Embankment and proceed to indulge in a riverfront singing game. The couple perform 'Pop Goes the Weasel', the traditional tune that Newley had taken into the British top twenty in 1961, to which the 'Tottenham sound' beat combo, in top hats and tails, respond with 'London Bridge is Falling Down'. Group and duo end up exchanging songs as they caper by one another in a kind of folk 'round'.

Eighteen months after the show, however, it was time for 'Ivan in America' and further refrains of that cloying nursery rhyme. Our Corporation representative, in the company of Harold King, travelled with four polished, mounted and inscribed pieces of London Bridge. By the end of their first press conference in New York the pair had probably already grown heartily sick of 'London Bridge is Falling Down'. But it was to be the core part of Luckin's sales pitch, and its familiar refrain, repeated over and over again in press releases, speeches and presentations, constantly enough to become almost bludgeoning, he trusted would be as invidiously effective as the catchiest advertising jingle. Still, by repeatedly mentioning the rhyme, rendered all the more timelessly ancient for being first heard in early childhood, he probably succeeded in distracting attention away from the relative youthfulness of the actual bridge up for sale.

After New York, Luckin and King and their team flew to Washington, where they held another press conference and met the British ambassador, Sir Patrick Dean. Previously Britain's representative at the United Nations, Dean had the unenviable job of representing London in Washington in the closing half of the 1960s, as the Vietnam War escalated. Dean had taken up the post in 1965, the year when Lyndon Johnson's re-elected Democratic administration began to massively increase American military activity in the region. Johnson had then declared: 'If we don't stop the Reds in South Vietnam . . . next week they will be in San Francisco' – and by 1968 there were over half a million US troops in Vietnam. Johnson, extremely sensitive to criticism, held a low opinion of foreign ambassadors at the best of times. But the British government's reluctance to commit ground forces to a war that as a loyal ally it felt duty bound to publicly support but privately considered misguided, meant Dean was required to perform some rather adroit diplomatic footwork.*

If the American president was unhappy with the British government, then a section of the British public was not exactly enamoured

---

* Once asked why he did not take a stronger line against the war in Vietnam when disquiet over the conflict was growing among his own backbenchers, Harold Wilson is said to have replied, candidly, 'Because we can't kick our creditors in the balls.'

of the American administration either. And within days of Luckin and King landing in America, and a week exactly after Crosby's article on the sale had run in the *Observer*, London saw the biggest anti-Vietnam war demonstration to date in Britain.* Thousands of young protesters, the writer and activist Tariq Ali and the actor Vanessa Redgrave at their head, marched from Trafalgar Square to the American embassy in Grosvenor Square, some carrying banners and chanting 'Ho-Ho-Ho Chi Minh! Hey, Hey LBJ, how many kids did you kill today?' At the Embassy they were met by ranks of police on foot and horseback and, according to the *Guardian* newspaper, 'a few hundred Conservatives and Monday Club supporters who shouted such slogans as "Bomb, bomb the Vietcong" and "Treason".' Scuffles broke out and a pitched battle duly ensued, with demonstrators lighting firecrackers, throwing bottles and stones and flailing out against charging mounted officers, and many a police truncheon, fist and boot making contact with the head of a protester – as archive film footage confirms. Some 300 people were arrested, fifty people, including policemen, were taken to hospital and thirteen of the embassy's windows were broken.

With even the dear old BBC soon beaming images of the Nice (whose live stage act frequently concluded with an American flag being set ablaze) tearing through their rock-instrumental 'protest' version of Leonard Bernstein's 'America' – with keyboardist Keith

---

* And though not made public until the following year, it was also over the same weekend that American soldiers in Charlie Company gunned down over 500 Vietnamese civilians – men, women and children – in just three hours at My Lai.

Emerson gaily plunging knives into his Hammond organ as the nation in near-unison tucked into their tea – Luckin's and King's visit presented the British Diplomatic Service with a welcome chance to reassert the 'specialness' of Anglo-American relations. And after a few days wining, dining and glad-handing in the American capital, Luckin and King departed again, this time for the West Coast and Los Angeles, where two local businessmen seemed especially anxious to discuss a proposition they had in mind.

CHAPTER 9

A Message from Disney Time

Cornelius Vanderbilt Wood Jnr, known almost universally as 'Woody', was particular about chilli – or 'the Bowl of Red', as this incendiary dish is still known in the state of Texas, where he was raised. His own recipe – and Woody was twice crowned World Champion at the annual International Chili Society's Cookoff, established at the remote Texan ghost town of Terlingua in 1967 – calls for four pounds of canned tomatoes, eight ounces of Budweiser beer, three pounds of stewing chicken, four pounds of flank steak, five pounds of pork chops, six green chillies, two green peppers, suet, garlic, cumin, oregano, thyme and coriander. And two days, preferably three, of patient frying, simmering, leaving overnight, reheating and finishing off with a sprinkling of jack cheese and limejuice into the bargain. Though no beans, never beans.

For Woody, chilli with beans was an insult to the frontiersmen who carried dried beef and peppers to stew with water on the trail west. Easterners, like those fools in Cincinnati adding cloves, cinnamon, cocoa, kidney beans and spaghetti (for gawd's sake!), would never understand. Meat and pepper: for Texans it was like the transubstantiation and bread and wine. A mouthful and you

were communing with cattle drivers on the Chisholm Trail or
transported to the years when San Antonio's plazas were crowded
with chilli vendors, their pots bubbling away on open fires. Why
his Beverly Hills neighbour, Dave Chasen, the vaudeville hoofer
turned restaurateur to the stars, felt compelled to add pinto beans
remained a mystery to Woody. He'd ribbed him about it often
enough. Though with Elizabeth Taylor having quarts of the stuff
flown out frozen to the set of *Cleopatra* in Rome, and Frank
Sinatra, Orson Welles, Johnny Carson, Harold Ross and Ronnie
Reagan all fawning over it, Woody guessed his friend could afford
to ignore this particular word to the wise. And after a forkful of
Chasen's speciality 'Hobo' steak, a three-inch-thick fillet seared
in butter at the table and served on toasted sourdough bread,
Woody usually found himself willing to overlook Dave's folly
over the beans – more so once he'd first seized the Cookoff
crown. In the eyes of the world, the small world, admittedly, of
chilli aficionados, and anyone who had glanced at the *LA Times*
on the day that a full-page ad declaiming his victory had run, he
was the best. Or as he liked to put it, exaggerating an already
pronounced south-western drawl, the 'UndeFeeted UndeniaBull
World's Champion'.

By then, however, he'd already notched up plenty of other
titles, among them 'the Man Who Moved London Bridge', 'the
Creator of the World's Largest Fountain', and 'the Designer-
Builder of Disneyland' – although promulgation of the latter

resulted in Walt Disney issuing a suit against him and even now one can search in vain for a mention of his name in any official history of the animator's amusement park. But he was there in that sandy orange grove in Anaheim, California, back in 1954. Thirty-three years old, tall, loquacious, a champion lariat twirler, alumnus of Oklahoma University with a major in petroleum engineering and the director of an aviation firm during the war, Woody was poached by 'Uncle' Walt from the Los Angeles economics department of the Stanford Research Institute, where he'd compiled the feasibility study for Disney's park, to be general director of the project.

Remembered by one former associate from that time as 'the most winning and likeable personality one could expect to find', he charmed Disney with his intelligence, down-home manner and competence, the older man treating him like a son at the outset. But within months of Disneyland's troubled but ultimately validating opening and with visitors flocking in, the creator of Mickey Mouse had Woody sacked and assumed control of running the park himself.* To this day, rumours, ranging from accusations of embezzlement to paranoia that Woody was simply getting too big for his boots, continue to fly around this decision, but no satisfactory reason has ever been given for the dismissal. However, Disney was notorious for finding delegation impossible and had a long track record of turning on the very people he'd originally empowered to lessen his workload.

Undeterred, Woody formed a contracting firm for the amusement industry, Marco Engineering, and waving three fingers at his ex-boss went about luring former Disney colleagues away to design a string of rival parks. The first, Magic Mountain in Golden, Colorado, opened in 1959 – and closed less than a year later. His next two creations (billed, much to Walt's ire, as 'the Disneylands of the East'), Pleasure Island at Wakefield, Massachusetts, and Freedomland in the Bronx, New York, fared little better. The poor New England summer weather by all accounts did for Pleasure Island, though it clung on for a decade, life-sized model Moby Dick whale, pirate galleon and all. Freedomland, on the other hand, occupying the old mosquito-infested Pelham Bay rubbish dump from 1960, turned out to be a rather classic example of overestimating public taste.

Laid out like a map of the United States, the park was themed

---

* And the opening was a horror of wet asphalt, half-finished buildings, vast (uninvited) crowds, waterless drinking fountains and disastrously shambolic live TV coverage involving Ronnie Reagan.

around the history of America – with a brief excursion to the
nation's future new frontier: outer space – and gave little Biff
and Linda the chance to sail on a New Orleans stern-wheel
riverboat, help douse the Great Chicago Fire and savour some
of those good vibrations from the San Francisco earthquake.*
With the bicentennial on the horizon, it expected to coin it in,
but was judged a little too pedagogical for most. Especially when
there were the thrills of Rockaways' Playland with its Atom
Smasher rollercoaster to be had over in Queens. In any case, the
park was soon bang up against the 1964–5 New York World's
Fair exhibition, the massive trade and industry jamboree, on
nearby Flushing Meadow, for which Woody had produced a
'global' pavilion for Coca-Cola featuring replicas of the temple
of Angkor Wat in Cambodia and Rio's Copacabana Beach.†
Freedomland shut, bankrupt, at the end of the 1964 season.
However, the Six Flags Over Texas Park in Arlington, drawn up
by Woody for local property mogul Angus G. Wynne, and which
opened in 1961, was popular enough to lead to a wider franchise,
and still exists in a modernised form today.

---

* And here there does seem to be an uncanny similarity between Freedomland's
  map-shaped layout and theme and Brian Wilson of the Beach Boys' equally
  ill-fated concept album *Smile* – a record conceived as a track-by-track
  quasi-historical journey across America.

† Pepsi-Cola's pavilion at the same fair, meanwhile, was the work of Disney
  and boasted a continent-squeezing Grand Tour ride, with voyagers able to
  glide past an animated scene of 'the changing of the guard at Buckingham
  Palace, beneath English carollers on a crescent moon and amid tulips and
  windmills of Amsterdam'.

It was also in 1961 that Woody merged his Marco operation with a firm belonging to Robert Paxton McCulloch, another Los Angeles-based entrepreneur he'd first met on the construction site of Disneyland.

And it was Robert P. McCulloch whom Woody rang one night early in 1968, to inform him that they'd be buying London Bridge.

Woody was in New York at the time with William Zeckendorf Jnr, the property developer involved in the consortium who'd snared the *Queen Mary* for Long Beach and more latterly also approached the Corporation of London about London Bridge. McCulloch received the call in Los Angeles and, with the time difference and knowing his associate's convivial nature, assumed Woody 'was drunk'. He later recalled thinking he'd have to 'get out there . . . to bail him out'. But Woody, having convinced McCulloch that he was sober, or sober enough, made it plain that he was completely serious and outlined his plan. In the light of everything else they were doing, the apparent insanity of what he suggested struck McCulloch as perfectly sane.

As indeed it might for Messrs McCulloch and Wood of McCulloch Properties Inc., a subsidiary of the McCulloch Oil Corporation of California, as the McCulloch Corporation were developing a brand-new city in twenty-six arid square miles of the Mojave Desert in Arizona – a 'Great American Nowhere' that had previously only nurtured cactus, mesquite and paloverde. It was a venture to which Woody himself, when first shown the proposed site and invited to come on board by McCulloch in the fall of 1960, had responded, bluntly, 'Bob, you're out of your mind.' And whatever R. D. Laing was then up to with anti-psychiatry and *The Divided Self*, both men were soon to grow rather accustomed to being labelled mad.

Robert Paxton McCulloch was born in 1911 in St Louis, Missouri. Also the birthplace of T.S. Eliot, St Louis was then the fourth largest city in America and a thriving industrial and cultural metropolis on the Mississippi that had hosted the 1904 Olympic Games. Descended from a family of wealthy Midwestern industrialists, McCulloch was linked by marriage to the Wisconsin motor-manufacturing giants, Briggs & Stratton. He studied engineering at Stanford and Princeton, along with indulging a passion for high-speed boating that saw him scoop two national championship trophies for outboard hydroplane racing – the aquatic equivalent of Formula One. Devoting his energies and not inconsiderable inherited wealth to various mechanical enterprises after graduation, by the age of thirty he had sold his first racing engine and super-charger company in Milwaukee for $1 million. This Dr Evil-esque sum was agreed on the fly because McCulloch thought it sounded like a 'nice round figure'. Hailing from the same city as Lindbergh, McCulloch's next venture was an aviation company producing engines for military aircraft during the Second World War. But since even the *Spirit of St Louis* had been built in San Diego, he relocated to the West Coast after the war, buying up sixty-five acres of land near the then still modest Los Angeles Airport and setting up a string of new plants on Century Boulevard. Soon after that, McCulloch, whose favoured hour for starting to wrestle with any problem that took his fancy was 4 p.m. and who would often remain working at his desk until the following morning, perfected a more advanced supercharger for car engines. His Paxton Superchargers were later to be found under the bonnets of soupier models of Ford Thunderbirds – those T-Birds perpetually celebrated flying along the black-top in popular songs.

However, his real breakthrough was the creation of the first chainsaw light enough to be operated by a single person. No forest, log, block of ice or gang of teenagers camping out in an abandoned farmhouse* were ever quite as safe again after the McCulloch 3-25 landed in hardware stores in 1949. Having made the distant whinny and putt-putt of buzz saws as familiar to American summers as willow on leather in England, he then diversified into oil exploration, publishing and property with the Thunderbird Valley Estate

---

* Only in movies, obviously. I am not implying that McCulloch models were used in any real-life massacres in Texas or anywhere else.

at Palm Springs and a marina at Lake Mead. Then, in 1957, he acquired the Scott–Atwater outboard-motor company of Minneapolis with the aim of shifting production to California.

Not unlike John Rennie, McCulloch was forever fiddling around with some new wild idea – one of his near-misses in the 1960s was the Gyroplane, a hybrid airplane–helicopter so compact it could slide into any suburban twin-garage. He also shared the great man's restless quest for mechanical perfection. So, while Scott–Atwater outboard motors were probably fine for Cliff Scott and H. Bruce Atwater, they weren't, in his opinion, good enough to bear the name McCulloch. To improve the models that would be built under his imprimatur, the chainsaw king wanted to establish a test centre near the plant. Initially, R&D was conducted at Redondo Beach, California. But for his outboard motors to clean up they needed to perform well in freshwater lakes. And as no suitable site was available in Los Angeles, he began to scout further afield.

On St Patrick's Day 1958, and under the auspices of his corporate pilot Jim Darley, who knew the terrain from Air Force days of old, McCulloch flew from Palm Springs over the Mojave Desert. Flying by the Colorado River and between the rough desert peaks of western Arizona, Darley brought their D18 Beechcraft plane down low, suddenly hovering above a long, narrow, bluey-green lake encroached by a jagged outlying peninsula and framed by the Chemehuevi Mountains in the distance: Lake Havasu. The presence of two tatty but functional airstrips and seven barracks dating from the Second World War, a covered boat dock and a small grocery store, Vic Spratt's cookhouse bar-restaurant and a smattering of other buildings, made it appear a viable enough locale for a spot of outboard-motor testing. Still, the lake was remote, at the further reaches of a dead-end road running some twenty-one miles off Route 66. The nearest town, Needles, over the state line in California, was more than thirty miles away. But McCulloch unfurled his chequebook and wasted no time in picking up over 3,500 acres, roughly six square miles, of lakeside land for $300,000.

The sellers, on the whole, couldn't quite believe their luck. Of course, they'd miss the fishing. Bass were plentiful, with nine-and-a-half-pound whoppers a regular haul. But the lake's peninsular, Pittsburg Point, used as a convalescence centre for the Army Air Corps during the Second World War and known in its years of active service as Site Six, was a $2 a night excuse for a resort, visited and run mainly by ex-service types and anglers. Among them was the actor Robert Taylor, who starred alongside Vivien Leigh in the transatlantic tearjerker *Waterloo Bridge* and treasured the privacy of Site Six's out-of-the-way location. Think of a roughed-up hillbilly version of the Columbia Inn in *White Christmas*, fiddle with the thermostat, add a stubby grove of salt cedar trees and the constant and unwelcome attention of skunks, wild horses and bobcats and we are somewhere near the mark. Pittsburg Point, like the lake, though, owed its existence to the building of the Parker Dam in 1938.

As anyone who has seen Roman Polanski's fictional tale of irrigation, murder and incest, *Chinatown*, will half know, securing a stable water supply for the burgeoning city of Los Angeles was a major political issue in the 1920s and 1930s. It led to the formation of the Metropolitan Water District of Southern California, with the real-life Hollis Mulwray, William Mulholland, designing the Colorado River Aqueduct, completed in 1935, and the Parker Dam to bring water over the mountains from Arizona into California. Observing the lake created by the dam – and Parker was to bury the old mining communities of Chemehuevi and

Liverpool under several feet of its water – two Native Americans, the 103-year-old Haranai and his 98-year-old wife, Oach, are reputed to have asked 'what magic' had turned their age-old 'red river' (literally in Spanish, 'Colorado') to a 'clear sparkling blue', and blue in the Mojave tongue is 'havasu'.

McCulloch would later claim that the instant he saw those glistening waters, he vowed there and then to found a new city on the shores of Lake Havasu. Whatever the truth of this, it was, rather like the creation of the lake itself, the expanding needs of Los Angeles that persuaded McCulloch to contemplate building his own city here – an act that most would consider a touch hubristic, to put it mildly. When he had first set up shop in Los Angeles, Pacific Electric 'Red Cars' traversed the city. Pan Am planes landed at handier-for-Hollywood Burbank (now Bob Hope) Airport rather than the Municipal Los Angeles Airport out on the coast at Westchester (along with McCulloch's factory). And the Dodgers remained at Ebbets Field in Brooklyn. In 1940, the city's population had stood at a mere 1,504,277. But by 1960 it was 2,479,015 and rising as fast as the new suburban tract homes constructed to accommodate the influx could be laid out. Then, following the debut of commercial jet flights in the early 1950s, it was decided to completely rebuild Los Angeles Airport.

Where previously graduates returning from eastern schools were left to pound the scalding tarmac avoiding jack rabbits to reach the terminal, from 1961 jetways, escalators and moving walkways whisked them around a series of hygienic concourses at the all new

International Airport – or LAX. At its centre stood the fly-me-to-the-moon Theme Building, a 900-ton steel structure like a visiting Martian saucer which housed an observation platform and a restaurant.*

But more mundanely, down on planet Earth, the airport's expansion was accompanied by a series of new municipal zoning arrangements that dictated what kind of businesses could operate in each area of the city. These tended to give priority to hotels and office blocks in the immediate vicinity of the airport and taxed existing industries heavily. Soon an acre around LAX was changing hands for $350,000 a pop and McCulloch's holdings had become simply too valuable to be left to manufacturing. With developers such as Marvin Kratter all but inviting him to name a price, McCulloch had to explore the possibility of moving his chainsaw plant elsewhere. Kansas City, Denver, Wichita and Phoenix were all jockeying to have one of his factories in their midst. But having by now established his test centre for outboard motors at Lake Havasu, the notion of founding his own town, his own city, in this distant quarter of Arizona took on a kind of logic. What better place to build his factory? And with his factory, he had the starter yeast of a whole commercial real-estate proposition – one that in retrospect always appeared conceived more in the vein of Bailey Park

---

* At its opening ceremony in June 1961, Najeeb E. Halaby from the Federal Aviation Authority told the *Los Angeles Examiner* newspaper that the new airport 'may well achieve some of the worldwide renown . . . as – who knows – Disneyland'. In the 1990s, a team from Disney's 'Imagineering' department would be brought in to renovate the building.

than Pottersville in Frank Capra's seasonal cinematic staple *It's a Wonderful Life*, but a potentially highly profitable enterprise all the same. And McCulloch certainly knew how to make money. At this point, his conglomerate was grossing $75 million a year and new towns, and new suburban housing estates, were a boom area. But perhaps a deeper psychological appeal was that by colonising this unclaimed quarter of the West for civilisation, McCulloch was seizing the opportunity to be at one with America's great pioneers.

Writing about the so-called hippie communes that sprang up somewhat later in the 1960s, William Hedgepeth singled out mobility as 'an unofficially admired' facet of the American character, noting that in a land 'settled by disgruntled transients', some forty million people, a fifth of the population then, 'changed their place of residence every year'. Citing the enduring allure of the frontier, he continued: 'There had persisted in people's minds the sensation that the nation is always on the brink of something bigger. And along with this Americans have forever sensed a mystic beckoning from the sheer enormity of the land itself, whose boundless newness seems to offer constant hope of ever better things beyond, just up ahead.'

Most of the 'hippies' sharing peace and love, mung-bean stew, bongs, sexual partners, bodily fluids and venereal diseases in the geodesic domes of Drop City, Colorado, say, would probably not have welcomed being compared to the inhabitants of a community put together by a 'bread-head' corporation. But these inhabitants were not so radically different to the band of 'city-weary Americans, restlessly looking for a change', in the summation of one early resident, who upped sticks for Lake Havasu.

Like the 'Somewhere' sung about in *West Side Story*, packing out movie houses as McCulloch marched on with his scheme, Lake Havasu would offer a new way of living. Open air, peace and quiet, room to breathe, a big sky, scenic mountains, a hot dry climate, cool blue water, good fishing, and for a humble sum, a piece of rocky earth you could call your own.

Nevertheless it was nearly four frustrating years before McCulloch and Woody acquired the twenty-six square miles they required to build their city. By 1963 over $500,000 had already gone on advance planning. Woody, after crunching numbers, scouting the terrain by air, boat and on the roadless ground in a four-wheel drive, pored over charts and maps, and actually thumbed through telephone directories of other long-standing cities to determine what local businesses – from bakers to bowling alleys – would be vital for a community of their estimated size to thrive. He then drew up blueprints for a free-standing community with an economy based on forty per cent tourism, twenty per cent retail and municipal services and forty per cent light industry.

Following what one local historian politely refers to as 'considerable finagling', McCulloch was able to buy some 13,000 acres of federal land, originally allocated for schools, from the state of Arizona at a public auction in August 1963. A month later, Mojave County recognised Lake Havasu as 'an official Irrigation and Drainage District' and therefore 'a municipal corporation for all purposes'. North of the lake, however, a vista of eight dusty bare miles of rocks and sand, dotted with greasewood and tules, was all that greeted anyone choosing to visit the municipality at this point. After gesturing in the direction of various ranges of scrubby dust, where he assured a party of understandably somewhat incredulous visitors in November 1963 that hotels, homes, churches and shopping centres would soon rise, Woody memorably concluded his sales pitch by pronouncing Lake Havasu 'Palm Springs with water'. And in earnest, by all accounts, as later 11,000 palm trees were imported from California.

From January 1964, and in contrast to some of the other sight-unseen deals on offer at that time, McCulloch launched a fly-before-you-buy scheme that lasted until 1978. In total some 137,000 potential settlers who paid a modest deposit were flown free of charge out to Lake Havasu in a fleet of eleven Lockheed planes. And, with the construction, at an area known as Copper Canyon, of the Nautical Inn, with its 180-seater dining room and plush cocktail lounge, they were able to have a pretty gay time, eating, drinking, boating and fishing on the lake over a weekend and all courtesy of McCulloch, as they soaked up the atmosphere and chewed over the prospect of moving out there.

In addition to the inn, by the end of 1964 the new chainsaw plant (costing $2 million) was up and running along with a smattering of apartments and office buildings, a shopping centre called the Arnold Plaza (replete with a Claypool's supermarket), the Standard gas station, an elementary school and a purpose-built suburb (to a still rather underpowered 'urb') of ranch-style tract homes for McCulloch employees. Within a further eighteen months, a full fifty miles of street had been paved. Prayers could be said at the First Southern Baptist Church. Boats moored and fishing tackle bought at the marina. Steaks eaten at Crazy Ed's sawdust-floored and necktie-festooned diner. Beers sunk at Ron's Rustic Inn tavern on the newly completed McCulloch Boulevard. Ailments inspected at Dr Daniel Blez's surgery, although those in need of surgery had a forty-mile trek to Kingman. Teeth pulled at Dr Hal Torgerson's dental practice and money extracted from the Valley National Bank. By then the city had already witnessed its first marriage when schoolteacher Geraldine McGuire and her beau Kenneth Stevens tied the knot on a pontoon boat in the middle of the lake. And its first robbery, with two men holding up the liquor store on Arnold Plaza and speeding away with $451 from the cash register. Which given that an average six-pack of beer was yours for 99 cents back then and that officially only 1,037 men, women and children were currently calling Lake Havasu home, perhaps indicates a healthy intake of fluids in this dusty place.

To promote Lake Havasu, McCulloch and Woody hired their own Don Draper in the form of seasoned Beverly Hills-based publicist Laurence 'Larry' Laurie. Also employed to help entice fresh-air-loving sporting types to the lake's burgeoning facilities was Clarence 'Gus' Newman, for twenty years the Outdoor editor of the *Los Angeles Examiner*. And so an annual bass fishing competition with generous cash prizes was established and a picture of a trio of Hollywood 'starlets', Cami Sebring,* E. J. Peaker and Celeste Yarnall, looking blissfully happy posing with rods by the lake, circulated to the national press. Later these were to be joined by no less endearing shots of beefy guys with well-chewed stubs of cigars in their smiling mouths, cradling fish that could have swallowed Jonah whole.

Upping the ante in 1966, Laurie and Newman presented the 'Outboard World Championship'– which, with its $25,000 top prize, they were able to plug as 'the World's Richest' outboard-motor-racing contest – and a visit by Dwight D. Eisenhower. Eisenhower was personal guest of honour of McCulloch, described by the *New York Times* as a 'frequent golfing partner of the former President'. Although now in frail health he seemingly warmed to Lake Havasu – as perhaps was to be expected from an ex-military man who was fond of hunting, fishing, a drink and the Western novels of Zane Grey.

In a speech at Columbia University in 1949, Eisenhower had heralded what he called 'the age of the individual', outlining a rather more cooperative version of 'rugged individualism' than of old, one that chimed rather well with the founding ethos of Lake Havasu, as he noted that there was 'no limit to the temporal goals we set ourselves – as free individuals joined in a team with our fellows'. Ike's belief in this empowered interdependency, for want of a better phrase, was perhaps best illustrated by his backing for

---

* Sebring was the ex-wife of celebrity hairdresser and later Manson murders victim Jay Sebring.

one of America's most significant programmes of public works – the creation of the interstate highway system with the passing of the Federal-Aid Highway Act of 1956. This legislation, by easing state-to-state transportation, played its own part in speeding up speculative developments much like Lake Havasu City across America and increasing suburban sprawl.*

Ike had something of a penchant for all things Western, once confessing to a White House aide that his favourite song was Bob Roberts' 'Ragtime Cowboy Joe'. And on that day at Lake Havasu, not far off Route 66, it seems implausible that this musical tale of an Arizona cowboy who serenades his herd with ragtime numbers wouldn't have occurred to Ike as he was wined, dined and entertained by McCulloch – who as an entrepreneur

---

* Ike's enthusiasm for this road-building project perhaps went back nearly a quarter of a century before the D-Day landings, and less than a year after the signing of the armistice ending the First World War. Ike, then a young lieu-tenant colonel, had joined the First Transcontinental Motor Convoy – an army expedition travelling from Washington to San Francisco. This coast-to-coast odyssey had shown that while it was possible to journey from one side of the nation to the other in large motor vehicles, it was far from painless with the famed transcontinental Lincoln Highway, a memorial to another Republican president, judged close to 'an imaginary line, like the equator'. In its wake, and with the car and car-manufacturing becoming a lynchpin of the American culture and economy, the federal government began a plan for improving national highways and inaugurated the numbering system that would bring Route 66 into being in the late 1920s. Arriving a decade after the road was immortalised in song by Bobby Troup and turned into a hit by Nat King Cole, Ike's Interstate scheme would actually act as its executioner in the end. But back in 1966, there probably wasn't a roadway more identifiably American than Route 66. Thanks to Troup, its name, even when intoned by Mick Jagger in a voice that owed more to Dartford than the Oklahoma Dust Bowl, had become shorthand for life, liberty and the pursuit of happiness on wheels.

represented a figure that had superseded the cowboy in the national iconography.

For here, despite its new factory plants and luxury motel, was a classic frontier desert town. It was just a few years old, had no municipal government and only a volunteer firefighting service. Coyotes howled into the night. Attempts to construct a road from Parker, twenty miles away, had been hampered by wild burros who developed an insatiable appetite for the wooden stakes and multi-coloured plastic marking ribbons laid by surveyors from the Arizona State Highway Department. Lizards frolicked in backyards only levelled by bulldozers months earlier. Visits by former presidents and world championship outboard-motor racing aside, its social whirl revolved around such homely pleasures as Saturday night Elk Club meetings, church on Sunday, ribs with a cold beer and a jaw at Ron's bring-your-own barbeque, a shindig to Smokey Rogers and his music group at the Nautical Inn, and the cooking of freshly caught fish over a campfire on the lakeside with friends. As far as its geography, attitudes, tastes and whole demeanour went, Lake Havasu was as unquestionably and resolutely American as anywhere in the States.

Arguably more so, as the British statesman, historian and, later, ambassador to the United States Viscount Bryce had written in 1888: 'The west is the most American part of America: that is to say, the part where those features which distinguish America from Europe come out in the strongest relief.' Frederick Jackson Turner was subsequently to quote Bryce's opinion, admiringly, in his seminal 1893 essay on the West, 'The Significance of the Frontier in American History'. Turner himself went on to maintain that 'the separation of Western man from the seaboard, and his environment, made him to a large degree free from European precedents and forces. He looked at things independently and with small regard for appreciation for the best Old World experience.'

As an emblem of this westward-gazing spirit, then, Lake Havasu didn't look like the kind of settlement in the market for a pile of old stones from England.

However, this new city did, as it happens, need a bridge. In 1962, McCulloch and Woody had commissioned the Tri-Co Engineering company to survey the area and report back on any flooding or drainage issues. A particular concern that cropped up, and an issue that was to become increasingly pressing as more folk ventured out on to the lake and moved into the area, was the build-up of stagnant water at the Thompson Bay part of the lake. This stemmed from the fact that Pittsburg Point was partially blocking the downstream flow of Lake Havasu. To correct this Tri-Co advised digging a channel through the isthmus that joined the peninsula to the mainland. But if this solved the problem of stagnant water it would also somewhat obviously separate the peninsula from the mainland, turning it into an island. And the easiest solution to that was to build a bridge over this new channel.

McCulloch and Woody, apparently hedging their bets for a couple of years while deciding exactly what action to take, could easily have put up a new bridge. They had a new *city*, after all. Albeit one whose resident population for now hovered at about a tenth of the number of pedestrians filing over London Bridge in a single rush hour. McCulloch had envisaged some 90,000 people living at Lake Havasu City in the end. And while lots were ticking over nicely enough, there was a feeling that four years in an added push to sales was required. Without that there lurked the fear that the whole enterprise could stall, or worse, flounder completely at this crucial embryonic phase. Identity was felt to be even more of an issue. Lake Havasu had a great lake. And one that was bound to get much better once they sorted out the stagnant water at Thompson Bay. Nobody could deny that. But then so did Duluth, Minnesota. Topock Gorge was certainly majestic. Still, was Havasu more majestic than the Grand Canyon? A desert water resort was an appealing enough prospect. Was it as appealing, though, as Palm Springs, say? And on it went.

But from the second Zeckendorf let slip that London Bridge

was up for sale in 1968, Woody knew he had stumbled upon the answer to their prayers. In a single stroke, unsanitary algae could be banished from Thompson Bay and Lake Havasu would gain a unique, historic feature, a talking point to put this new (and as yet un-incorporated) city on the world map. Did it matter that much of that conversation was of the incredulous 'What the blazes?', 'Are you drunk/insane?' variety. Not really. For the time being procuring it alone remained the most pressing thing. To that end, lunch was arranged in Los Angeles with Woody and Gus Newman meeting Ivan Luckin and Harold E. King.

The City representatives were by this time also being courted by at least one other West Coast consortium. It was fronted by the Hollywood comedian Red Skelton and their plan, as far as can be gathered, involved transforming the bridge into a theatre-cum-entertainment venue in Palm Springs. Luckin, never averse to hobnobbing with the stars, could hardly have been disappointed with their interest. Nevertheless, it appears he and King struck up an easy rapport with Woody in particular. King and Woody were both in effect town planners with their individual store of anecdotes about the logistics of getting grand projects up and keeping them running. Luckin and Woody, on the other hand, shared a mutual love of gimmicks and showmanship, relishing any possibility to cause a bit of a stir in the press. With his Texan drawl and idiomatic turn of phrase – male acquaintances were frequently addressed as 'Dad' or 'Daddyo', women 'honey' or 'sugar', while 'Well I be dog-goned' was a commonly deployed expression of wonder or surprise – Woody couldn't help but make an impression on the Englishmen. After lunch, Luckin and King were flown directly out to Lake Havasu, where they were treated like visiting royals and soft-soaped with hard sell. Back in Los Angeles, they met the chainsaw king himself, or 'our fearless leader', as Woody customarily introduced McCulloch – this typically condensed to 'Fearless' when the two men were jibing each other. Pale-suited and wearing saddle shoes, a footwear adopted since college days and a sartorial flourish that implied an on-the-move good-to-go sportiness (or, alternatively, corns and/or wide feet), McCulloch was businesslike and discussions about the conditions of the sale continued until 11 p.m. that evening. The following morning, Luckin and King flew east to New York for a final round of meetings and press interviews before heading home to London.

According to Gus Newman, over the course of that day together, much of Woody's substantial energies had been devoted to coaxing some sense of a likely winning figure out of Luckin and King. The Brits, perhaps fearing a dispute of the kind that had erupted over the *Queen Mary*, refused to be drawn, keeping as inscrutably vague on the matter of finance as any beneficiary of the Civil List. But Woody, after hours of wheedling, did eventually succeed in obtaining an estimate for the cost of dismantling the bridge – the amount quoted was $1,200,000. Beginning with this sum, Woody and McCulloch later agreed that a hundred per cent profit was a probably decent enough return for the City and had all but decided to offer $2,400,000 for the bridge. (This, of course, implies that contrary to the Corporation's many claims when they first put the bridge up for sale, some profit was expected.)

In the midst of Woody's and McCulloch's discussion, for reasons that are anyone's guess – and who knows, perhaps spending the previous evening listening to Luckin yak on about Peter de Colechurch never living to see his creation become 'one of the wonders of the medieval world' triggered thoughts about mortality – McCulloch apparently started talking about his birthday. McCulloch was fifty-six, soon to be fifty-seven. By his calculation, if they won the bridge, then by the time they had the damn thing shipped over and reassembled at Lake Havasu he would be sixty years old. 'Dog-goned, you are right, Fearless,' or words to that effect, Woody is supposed to have replied, 'then let's bid an extra $1,000 for each year of your age.' And that, inexplicably, is what they did. Or so the story goes. Reverse-engineered or not, their final bid was indeed for $2,460,000. Or in pre-decimalisation (if post-devaluation) sterling: £1,029,400 10s 4½d – about £13.5 million in 2012. Ker-ching.

The deal was in effect clinched in New York on 23 March 1968 at Essex House, the swish art-deco hotel on Central Park South just off 7th Avenue. In Luckin's written recollection of the sale, he and King met Woody only a few hours before they were due to fly back to the UK. Composed some thirteen years after the event and for the ears of the American public, the account has

Luckin doing a full-on Willy Loman, clasping hands, looking Woody straight in the eye and uttering lines like 'You can get perfectly good stone down the road in California . . . I am selling history, sir, two thousand years of it', etc. Whatever went on in that hotel room, Woody lodged the bid. Six days after that the competition officially closed and all the tenders were totted up. Three weeks later the Corporation of London announced that Lake Havasu had seen off all the other contenders and would be the new home of London Bridge.

'I was very pleased and satisfied', Harold King reported at the time, in the tones of a mildly dotty headmaster handing out the end-of-year prizes,

when the tender accepted by the Bridge House Estates Committee in the sum of $2,460,000 was the sum submitted by the company who in my opinion had the best scheme for reuse. This company, the McCulloch Oil Corporation, whose proposed bridge site in Arizona we had visited during our stay in Los Angeles, proposed to reuse the London Bridge stone in facing a new bridge within a town development (all by private enterprise) situated along the Colorado River at a place called Lake Havasu City, an attractive area of Arizona being recovered from the desert to be used to house some 100,000 people in a new self-supporting city. The bridge will span from the mainland to a small island in Lake Havasu . . . This island to be created by severing the neck of a peninsula after the bridge has been rebuilt – a unique concept within a bold project, the satisfying creation of a living city from desert land.

How many other bids, if any, were really in serious contention is difficult to ascertain. In the States, only Red Skelton and his cohorts ever made their interest widely known – and it's not certain if they actually entered a tender when push came to shove. For some time to come, the Bridge House Committee meeting minutes covering the bidding process will remain confidential and the main players involved are now long dead. Luckin and King themselves never alluded to any other possible winner. But then both men were extremely satisfied with the Lake Havasu deal and their respective roles in brokering it. Although Luckin would come to denigrate King's contribution, telling the Arizona journalist Robert Johnson in 1981 that 'Harold King was strongly opposed to the idea of selling the bridge and was mainly involved as a technical advisor.' Whatever the truth of that, there was also another minor but noticeable difference between the two men's published comments about the sale. While King lent the Corporation's decision a veneer of nobility, extolling the power of private enterprise to raise cities from dust, Luckin referred to McCulloch as 'the highest bidder', inviting the conclusion it was the numbers that counted most of all to the City. Again this is strikingly at odds with the Corporation's earlier high-minded statements about 'no profit' being sought from the sale. But then, if someone is going to offer you double the costs, and bung a few thousand more into the bargain, you are hardly likely to turn it down, are you? And since London Bridge had for centuries been central to the City's wealth – and in the view of the archaeologist R. E. M. Wheeler, London as a settlement in effect began life as 'a parasite of London Bridge' – the opportunity to wring one last coin out of this loyal retainer was perhaps just too ingrained to resist.

Around the second week of April 1968, Woody, McCulloch and his son Robert Jnr, a company director, accompanied by the public-relations staffer Fred Melcher, came to London to finalise the deal. Robert Jnr, aided by Melcher, fielded many of the first round of interviews from British journalists once the news leaked on 18 April, a day before the official announcement, to the slight embarrassment of Larry Laurie who had been attempting to synchronise coverage over in the States.

The contract itself had already been signed, and with due ceremony, in the Guildhall on Tuesday the 16th – the day after Easter Monday, that year, which was marked by a CND rally against nuclear weapons and the Vietnam War in Trafalgar Square. Once pens were downed, Woody and McCulloch, Robert Jnr and Ivan trooped off to a lunch at the Mansion House hosted by the lord mayor, Sir Gilbert Inglefield. Later the Americans posed for photographs with Inglefield on their newly acquired bridge – a flurry of April showers requiring them to stand under umbrellas, which only added to the pictures' journalistic value.

In a week when *Firecreek*, a Western starring James Stewart as a humble farmer who dons a home-made sheriff's badge to defend his town from a gang of pitiless outlaws, opened at cinemas in the West End, the British press almost as one chose to marshal (no pun intended) almost every Cowboys and Indians cliché going to cover the story.* 'London Bridge Falls to the Apaches' ran the headline in the *Daily Express*, which noted that Rennie's crossing was to be rebuilt as a 'man-made rival to nature's spectacular Grand Canyon'. The *Evening Standard* had the bridge saddled up and 'Going West'. To be fair to the local hacks, the *New York Times* was not immune either, opting for 'Hey Geronimo! It's London Bridge'. Concluding rather more caustically, however, the *Guardian*, after reporting that the stones from the bridge were to be shipped from the Surrey Commercial Docks to Long Beach, California, and then trucked to Lake Havasu City, suggested that, 'perhaps some Briton should be at Long Beach to raise a bowler in salute as the dismembered corpse of London Bridge sails in past the hulk of the *Queen Mary*'. *The Times*, on the other hand, credited the purchasers with having pulled off a canny investment. In an article on 19 April headed 'Arizona's bargain buy' it reckoned that the bridge could 'bring millions' to the area and that Lake Havasu City expected to enjoy 'a 400 to 500 per cent' increase in visitor numbers once it was reassembled and *in situ*.

* Remarkably no journalist, it seems, picked up on a scene from another of that week's movie releases, *Planet of the Apes*, where a once famous landmark was depicted lying half-submerged in sand.

Over in the States, the sale and Woody and McCulloch were the subject of lengthy profiles in such glossies as *Life* and *Esquire*. For *Esquire*, the two men were interviewed by William Robbins in the famed Manhattan eaterie, and former speakeasy, the 21 Club, and persuaded to sketch out their plans for the bridge on one of the restaurant's white linen tablecloths – presumably with the establishment's consent.

The governor of Arizona, 'the Honourable Jack Williams', meanwhile sent a telegram of congratulations, in which he conceded there was a 'delightful irony in the fact that young, land-locked Arizona' was 'to be the new home for a world familiar structure' that had seen 'so much history swirl past it'. But, he argued, its presence would bring all the pageantry of history 'closer to millions of Americans' and 'bring a strong and happy surge of nostalgia to every person for whom "London Bridge is Falling Down" evokes the bright and problem-free days of childhood'.

The *Lake Havasu City Herald*, overegging as only proud natives can, maintained that it would 'be one of the most conspicuous deliveries from the Old World to the New World since the Statue of Liberty arrived from France in 1886'.

A noticeable absence across the board here, however, is even a passing mention of Tower Bridge.

CHAPTER 10

TB or Not TB

When Chelsea paid £50 million for Fernando Torres they got the worst deal London has seen since that American numbskull coughed up squillions for London Bridge, thinking he had bought Tower Bridge. (*Daily Mirror*, 16 March 2011)

Fakers on the make are, by popular consensus, two a penny in Los Angeles. But in 1938 this city of no angels was to lose one of the world's greatest with the death of Arthur Furguson. Like many inhabitants of that town, Furguson was an actor. Or had been. By the time he arrived in California, all his major performances were behind him. Born in Glasgow in 1883, he was the same age as Douglas Fairbanks Snr and only six years older than Chaplin. But never viewing moving pictures as anything other than gimmicky, he held screen acting in contempt, much preferring the non-take-twoness of the live stage. The theatre. That was the place to see real acting, he might occasionally say. Before adding, drolly, and with a chuckle at the thought of his finest roles and a mock-Shakespearean bow, 'But then all the world is a stage.' It was a hoary old line, as he well knew. And it was made no less hoary for being delivered with a wink and a nudge. But if anyone was justified in using it, Furguson believed, he was.

When was it that the idea of selling famous landmarks had first occurred to him? Had it been at the Hippodrome, or even the Playhouse, in Manchester, a few years after the Great War? Possibly. Though he was damned if he could remember the name of the show now. A dreary little comic ensemble, as he recalled. He was playing a gullible rich American in it, and rather well to his mind. As a native Scot, he had the rolling Rs down to a T and flailing about in a loud checked suit, exclaiming 'Gee whizz', he'd had the audience in fits. The plot, for what it was worth, revolved around his character being swindled out of his money – or 'dough' – by a wily Brit in a borrowed Harrow school tie. Odious Maurice Newton, was it? That old drunk. It was a miracle some nights he lasted through to the second act. Naturally Maurice's swindler got his comeuppance in the end, though most of the best lines on the way, and only a halfwit left thinking that Furguson's dumb Yank hadn't deserved it all along. Were there really such easy pickings out there? Americans with pocketbooks begging to be picked on the streets of London? Manchester? Birmingham? Carlisle? Humberside? Did Americans ever go to Humberside? It seemed unlikely. But London . . . Furguson was due down there soon enough – what would it hurt to take a closer look? And look he did. While other visitors to the capital ambled about gazing at the tidy formation of the changing of the guard, or the spiky Gothic of Westminster Abbey, Furguson spent his days studiously watching the sightseers themselves.

Having studied his prey, Furguson swooped in the summer of 1923. He picked out his first victim in Trafalgar Square, a prosperously, if preposterously, dressed American staring awestruck up at Nelson's Column. The maritime commander's monument, then a smudgy soot-black, as if inked in by Felix the Cat, and standing just shy of 170 feet above the square, retained its unhindered dominance over the West End skyline. Then as now, however, it remained a fixture, like a ship's mast, to which nervous tourists invariably lashed themselves in order to negotiate the choppy waters of a disorderly and confusing metropolis. And after striking up a conversation with the visitor as both men stood admiring the bronze frieze showing the young Nelson's victory at the Battle of St Vincent – the naval hero depicted in a pair of fetchingly snug breeches and a big swirly cape, receiving the surrender from a genuflecting Spaniard while semi-nude sailors, muscles rippling, tussle at his feet – Furguson knew he had snared the perfect greenhorn.

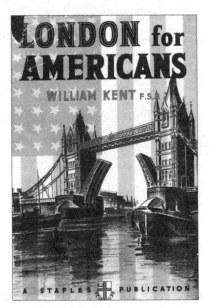

The man, apparently 'in corn' and from Iowa, seemed only too happy to believe that Furguson was working with the British government. And that the friendly, soberly attired stranger was charged with the task of settling war loans to America by selling off valuable national assets. Nelson's Column. The fountain. The four lions. This frieze and the other three, cast from cannons captured from the French during the Napoleonic period. It all had to go. From what the Iowan had already experienced of the plumbing, England quite obviously needed every penny it could get. But how much, he asked, fearing that his question would be perceived as embarrassingly crass, were the British government hoping to get for it? Oh, only about £7,000, perhaps £6,000 to a buyer, like the gentleman visitor himself, who truly appreciated the monument and would care for it properly, Furguson replied. The American, as intended, bought the compliment and before long had bought the Column, Furguson agreeing to deliver the deeds once the cheque had cleared. Come the agreed date to convene, though, Furguson was unexpectedly busy elsewhere. He was offloading Big Ben, as it happens, to another American who picked up London's celebrated timepiece for an almost criminally cheap £1,000. For Buckingham Palace, soon after that, he secured a down payment of £2,000. But after being inundated with complaints from Americans bearing emptied bank accounts and worthless bills of sale, Scotland Yard was on to him and Furguson judged it time to head overseas – and where better to try his luck than the United States?

Arriving on the East Coast in 1925, the year F. Scott Fitzgerald's *The Great Gatsby*, the tale of a charismatic millionaire with shady business dealings, was published, Furguson went about securing new tenants for the White House. The quite genuine death of President Coolidge's son from a septic infection incurred on the White House tennis courts provided him with a convincing enough reason for the sudden availability of this most prestigious address, the deposit a snip at $15,000.

As for the Statue of Liberty in New York . . . Well, as Furguson informed an Australian tourist who was under the impression he was being addressed by the city's district surveyor, it was a past-its-prime gift from the Old World. As fond as they'd become of it, and all that 'huddled masses' stuff, this was the Jazz Age. Gotham, he continued, was looking on and up. Had the Antipodean not seen the Shelton Towers Hotel on Lexington? The Paramount Building on Broadway? Or the Chrysler Building going up this very minute? Didn't they just knock that broad with the torch into a cocked hat? Besides, the New York Port Authority wanted to widen the harbour. Those guys, always with the big plans. Honestly. A tunnel under the Hudson here; a bridge over it there, Manhattan would be stitched tight to New Jersey before long. The city couldn't afford to get too sentimental about it, though. And the statue shouldn't be too difficult to box up and ship somewhere else. It had been done before, after all. Right now, the US State Department were open to offers from anyone willing to ferry it away. But Australia, Furguson added, as if never having considered the idea before, wouldn't that be something? The statue could be a baton passed from one young country to another, a symbol of their shared hopes for a brighter future, etc. The Australian, somewhat inevitably, agreed. It would, however, take him a little while to rustle up the money. Furguson grew impatient. The Australian suspicious. And the police were called.

A couple of years in prison, and Furguson headed west, where living off his carefully stashed wealth, the odd low-key fiddle here and there, and the kindness of budding young starlets, he finally died of a heart attack aged just fifty-five.

Or he would have done, probably.

Had he ever existed.

For while the story of his exploits, and in particular the sale of the capital's monuments to those damn Yankees with more money than sense, has become practically part of the Knowledge for London cabbies and subsequently chronicled in books like *Brewer's Rogues, Villains and Eccentrics*, and discussed on TV shows such as the BBC's *QI*, hard facts about Furguson and his cons are decidedly thin on the ground.

To an extent, that's not much of a surprise. Conmen, like hunters, are by profession compelled to cover their tracks and leave false trails. But scratching around for contemporary references to Furguson and his daring scams, Dane Love, the author of *The Man Who Sold Nelson's Column and Other Scottish Frauds and Hoaxes*, could unearth nothing concrete older than the 1970s. He also drew a blank on birth and death certificates, concluding in the end that the whole story was 'an urban folk tale'. Interestingly the formal notion of an urban myth itself hails from around the same period, with one of the earliest occurrences of the phrase 'urban legend' in its present meaning only appearing in print in 1968 – the year of London Bridge's sale.

Despite his tireless efforts, Love could not irrefutably disprove Furguson's existence, nor pinpoint the precise source of this urban folk tale – if that is what it is. But the Scot's modus operandi bears more than a passing resemblance to the antics of two rather more famous conmen, Robert C. Parker and Victor Lustig. And these tricksters, known respectively as The Man Who Sold the Brooklyn Bridge and The Man Who Sold the Eiffel Tower (Twice), at least had the decency to leave some verifiable documentation to accompany their nefarious activities.

Parker, known to have sold the Brooklyn Bridge for a piffling $50 on one occasion, and he sold it several times, also traded Grant's Tomb, Madison Square Garden and the Metropolitan Museum. Described at his fourth and final trial as 'an old-time confidence man' by the *New York Times*, he died in Sing Sing prison in 1936 having been incarcerated for life under the Baumes Laws eight years earlier for cashing a forged cheque in a Brooklyn restaurant. Lustig, originally from what is today the Czech Republic and who posed as an exiled Austro-Hungarian aristocrat, similarly passed away inside an American penal institution. He succumbed to pneumonia in Alcatraz in 1947, having already escaped from the Federal House of Detention in New York a few years earlier.

Lustig's reputation-making con, the sale, on two separate occasions, of the Eiffel Tower, was pulled off in the spring of 1925. At which point Furguson would presumably have still been at large in London. Intriguingly, in some versions of Furguson's biography, the Glaswegian is also credited with flogging the Eiffel Tower for scrap during a trip to Paris before departing for America. The idea of two people scamming the same monument virtually simultaneously is perhaps less far-fetched than it might at first seem. Over the years, many had tried their luck. In 1901, William McCloundy, aka IOU O'Brien, served two and a half years in Sing Sing for grand larceny having been apprehended selling the Brooklyn Bridge. Progressing to lots in City Hall Park, he, like Parker, also went down for life in 1928. In fact, by 1937 the Brooklyn Bridge ruse was such a hoary piece of Ye Olde New York lore as to be utilised in the plot of *Every Day's a Holiday*. This comedy set in the gay 1890s starred Mae West as a corset-and-bustle-clad con artiste, Peaches O'Day, who is banished from the city after stiffing a dumb rube of $200 for the bridge.

But, all of that said, the suspicion must surely remain that Furguson was dreamt up as a kind of Anglo-Celtic composite of these American models. In effect, Britain's answer to them and not far off Tommy Steele and Cliff Richard, say, in relation to Bill Haley and Elvis Presley during the heyday of rock'n'roll. Tales of wacky Americans buying up English churches, ocean liners and bridges and carting them off to Missouri, California or God knows where else, had by the early 1970s become almost monotonously predictable items on evening news bulletins.

But if such stories were usually treated to the comic 'And finally' slot, filling in where a visiting panda to London Zoo could not be coaxed out into the open or Ted Heath's yacht steadfastly refused to run aground, they hardly alleviated a growing fear that Britain was in inextricable decline.

With the economy deteriorating, inflation rising, output falling, worsening industrial relations, and an oil crisis or two still on the horizon, these were uncomfortable years for the nation, despite, if anything, further improvements in living standards for many ordinary people. After the flag waving of the 1966 World Cup and the camp (if American publishing and film industry sanctioned and funded) jingoism of Swinging London, there were only ignominious accusations of shoplifting, quarter-final defeat to Germany, metric currency and the dystopia of *A Clockwork Orange*.

In this fetid climate, and quite possibly soundtracked by a recording of 'Amazing Grace' by the Royal Scots Dragoon Guards that topped UK singles charts for five weeks in 1972, the urge to unearth, or arguably invent, a character like Furguson, a Scot who sticks it to loaded foreigners – Americans and, in some accounts of 'the myth', that evergreen British adversary, the French – becomes understandable, if never entirely forgivable. And it is this desire to salvage some national pride that clearly also oxygenated another urban legend that started to gain traction during this very same period: the belief that McCulloch and Co. had thought they were buying Tower Bridge.

Precisely when this particular myth – and I am afraid it is a myth, as we shall see – first took flight, is tricky to ascertain. By the early 1970s, it had already ossified into a truth universally acknowledged by gentlemen on bar stools up and down the capital. But the seeds of it were definitely germinating in 1968.

Of course, Tower Bridge, condemned by some commentators at its opening in 1894 as an 'architectural gimcrack' and 'a monstrous and preposterous architectural sham', was, and continues to be, the most recognisable of all London's bridges. From the beginning, its eye-catching twin-decks and *Ivanhoe*-esque turrets had the immediate advantage of photographing well, and easily, with the squeeze-box-bellowed plate-glass cameras available to Victorian smudgers. And it came into being at the instant when picture postcards, following a brisk trade in snaps of the Eiffel Tower at the Paris Exhibition in 1889, had developed into a fully blown craze.

The dissemination of its image over the following decades in photographs, motion pictures, newsreels, TV broadcasts, and on cheap souvenirs, ensured an international familiarity on a par with Big Ben – making it surprising that Furguson didn't, as far as we know, attempt to flog it in the 1920s. That it could be up for grabs in the late 1960s was not completely beyond the bounds of possibility either. Just after the Second World War a plan to redevelop it was mooted, and a scheme involving encasing the whole structure in glass, rather like double-glazing it perhaps, and creating 19,000 square metres of offices and housing did the rounds for several years following that. And two years after the London Bridge sale, by which point the St Katharine, the London and the Surrey docks had all closed, and with traffic on the Thames falling, the Planning and Communications Committee of the City Corporation issued a report exploring Tower Bridge's ongoing prospects. They noted that as 'only occasional users' on the river could 'be expected for the foreseeable future, such as ships forming part of a State occasion or visits by the Royal Navy or Foreign Navies, Training Ships, Yachts' the bridge should either be permanently closed and left as a road bridge or 'modernization' undertaken on the machinery so that it remained 'capable of being maintained and opened on an economic basis'. On the face of this, 'its future', writer John Pudney observed in 1971, was likely to be 'more decorative than practical'.

That Tower Bridge was, bluntly, far more decorative – and that is decorative as opposed to elegant – than Rennie's London Bridge, possibly rendered just too workaday by the diurnal stream of commuters, made the idea of purchasing the latter seem somehow unbelievable to most Londoners in 1968. 'I was often quizzed as to why anyone would wish to buy London Bridge,' King later confessed. 'The best answer', he stated, was one given to him 'by an American', who allegedly claimed 'that any other bridge in the world' was 'not worth a dime' but that London Bridge was 'something worth bidding for'. Which is hardly convincing.

But as Harold King's press statement makes plain, clearly some people who expressed an interest in the landmark quite genuinely did confuse London Bridge with its neo-Gothic neighbour – much as Google Images would do some forty-three years later. 'A surprisingly erroneous impression which had to be corrected throughout', King wrote, 'was that London Bridge was Tower Bridge, despite the fact that historically a London Bridge had been in existence since the first century whilst Tower Bridge is only 74 years old.'

Here, though, King seems to be referring to the sale at large, not to the winning bid per se, though I admit it is a touch ambiguous and could be (mis)interpreted that way.

Naïve confusions aside, Luckin's luxurious promotional brochure, in any case, proffered meticulous, stone by stone information about what prospective bidders would be buying. It had to, since only a fraction of the bridge's 130,000 tons of granite were actually up for grabs. And a percentage of that, as it happened, only dated from the widening in 1902, making parts of it younger than Tower Bridge.

As 'Drawing 3' in the booklet indicated, the stonework available 'for re-use as the facing to any arch bridge project of a similar shape and layout' consisted of '600 yards of balustrades weighing 500 tons and facing stonework with the supporting corbels to the balustrades weighing approximately 1,500 tons'. The arch spandrels, arch faces, cut waters and riverbank retaining walls weighed in at '8,000 tons' bringing the total weight of stonework for sale to 'approximately 10,000 tons'. And leaving one complete Rennie arch with a set of steps in place on the Surrey side of the Thames.

To ensure that all these pieces could be put back together again, as the bridge was being taken down the relevant stones were to be 'clearly marked with a number and plan prepared indicating the precise position of each numbered stone'. Prior to demolition, a comprehensive series of photographs were taken of all the balustrades, corbelling, voussoirs and cutwaters and so on, to supply a thorough visual guide to the bridge to help aid its reassembly – or recreation, really. And stone from the old bridge was to be ferried by barge to a special storage facility in the Surrey Commercial Docks, and diligently crated up in preparation for carriage or shipment to its new home. All of this was explained, and at length, in the brochure.

Essentially any new owner was buying an outer shell, inside which a new structure would have to fit, rather like a false nose and moustache in a fancy-dress costume, to create the impression of 'being' London Bridge. So, since you had, in effect, to build a bridge before you could put up your carry-out London Bridge, it's hard – though, not impossible – to see how anyone could not have known what they were buying.

McCulloch and Woody were, of course, busy guys with lots on their minds, diversifiers, multitaskers, restive prodders of fingers into whatever pies came within reach, who somehow still found time to knock up world championship chilli recipes and escort ex-presidents around golf courses. It is plausible, conceivably, that after treating King and Luckin to lunch in Los Angeles, flying them out to Lake Havasu and then flying them back to chew the fat about the bridge until 11 p.m. that night, and then later catching up with the City men again in New York at Essex House on 23 March 1968, to go over their final bid, that Woody, who was present throughout all these protracted sessions, and McCulloch, who dipped in and out, left still believing that Tower Bridge was on the table.

Sure, the bridge looked a little different, shorter, in the brochure Luckin had sent them. Less castle-like somehow, but then didn't everything look different in magazine spreads? Anyway, they'd probably stuck another storey on since then – bound to have done. Added the turrets and drawbridge and knocked through to make it a bit roomier. It all stood to reason . . .

All plausible, conceivably. Though only *just*.

In 1983, shortly before he died, Luckin rejected even the implication that the Americans were under any misapprehension about what they were purchasing. However, it is worth noting that around this same time Woody, having previously laughed off the story, suddenly began to suggest there might be something in it after all.

Booked as the guest luncheon speaker at a newspaper convention in Lake Havasu City in 1982, the Master Planner had been asked the inevitable question. Hadn't they bought the wrong bridge? To which, Woody, according to at least one attendee, replied: 'Yes, but so what if we did? It still worked.'

Versions of this confession, if confession was what it was, have been in circulation ever since. But how much of a mea culpa it amounts to remains open to debate. This was a press lunch and Woody was a past master of spinning a yarn to keep the notebook-carrying good ole boys in fedoras interested.

As we know, back in 1968, when Woody and McCulloch had come over to London to sign the contract, as part of the publicity drive surrounding the sale, they'd posed for a photo session with *Life* magazine on London Bridge. For this picture, and in the slightly goofy, knitting pattern models style of photojournalism that continued to hold sway in such periodicals, the dynamic duo, kitted out in slim-fitting suits and skinny ties, stood slightly apart on the bridge, linking the fingertips of their outstretched right arms. The resulting image is a loose imitation of the famous Sistine Chapel scene between God and Adam, restaged midway between Southwark and the City, with the viewer left to decide who is who or which is heaven and which is earth. (For the record, McCulloch, on the left of the photograph, stands on the City side.) This shot was to tally up in the magazine with a near-identical picture of the pair at the proposed location for the bridge in the desert by Lake Havasu. In the London photograph, however, by far and away the most striking detail, from our point of view, is that Tower Bridge is crash, bang, wallop, behind them.

In these circumstances, is it likely that sweat was gradually accumulating under their collars that cool, damp April afternoon, as the photo session got under way? Can we imagine Woody and McCulloch, perhaps, glancing around nervously as the photographer led them across the bridge? A few minutes passing as their aspiring David Bailey fiddled with his camera and lenses and got out his light meter before he finally ushered them into position in front of the balustrade. And all of that time, both men were occupied by a single thought. One that ran roughly like, 'Well I'll be dog-goned . . . aren't we supposed to be, you know, over there for this?' And having expressed it out loud, as politely as possible in this land of crust-less cucumber sandwiches and undrinkable coffee, the dreadful reality of their predicament would have become all too quickly apparent. What were they to do, though? There was no option but to tough it out. Be fearless, Fearless, it was too late now. And $2.5 million for a bridge they needed to cure their stagnant-water problem, was it really so much? They'd recoup on the publicity, easily, surely?

If this scenario is implausible, then it is conceivable that conversations like it might just possibly have occurred at an earlier point in the proceedings, perhaps after Woody and McCulloch had first met Luckin and King in the States. But it seems simply too preposterous to believe they flew into London expecting to tag, bag and ship Tower Bridge home.

But there is one further piece of evidence from their April 1968 trip – a piece left seemingly undisturbed for some forty years – that does most to lay to rest the Tower Bridge story. Though, intriguingly, it may equally be one of the earliest sources of the myth.

On 18 April 1968, McCulloch's son, Robert Jnr, recorded an interview for BBC Radio 4's longstanding current affairs programme *Today*. Although justly famed in recent decades for the quality of its news coverage and its gloves-off treatment of any politician with an indefensible policy to defend, in the late 1960s, *Today* remained more of a mañana, mañana. Hosted by the avuncular, witty but often erratic Jack de Manio – the names of African countries and reading out the correct time were peculiar stumbling blocks for the presenter – the show amounted to a couple of hours of topical chit-chat, and even the occasional poem slotted between bulletins, rather than a news programme as such. That said, it was still how several million Britons absorbed the main stories of the day as they jolted themselves into consciousness with tea and buttered toast. And there must have been the odd spluttering of hot liquid and choking fit on a half-chewed crust that morning as listeners heard Robert McCulloch Jnr inform a bemused de Manio that he would soon be re-erecting London Bridge on dry land.

Their amiable three-minute exchange began with de Manio gently probing McCulloch Jnr about the price. 'One million pounds by anyone's standard is an awful lot of dough and it seems an awful lot of dough to pay for something somebody didn't want,' he suggested. The American slang word 'dough' here was pronounced with deliberate overemphasis and rendered all the more jarring for twice being preceded by an 'awful' that contains vowel sounds seldom heard anywhere outside the Royal Enclosure at Ascot after about 1980. In response McCulloch Jnr trotted out the line about their winning bid being calculated to include $60,000 for his father's approaching birthday, though he also managed to draw some pertinent comparisons between Lake Havasu City and Britain's new towns. But it is at the interview's finale that McCulloch Jnr made, for the topic to hand, his most revealing statement.

Pondering the loss to America of the *Queen Mary*, the *Queen Elizabeth*, and now London Bridge, de Manio concluded by asking his guest whether he had his 'eye on anything else? A bit', he goaded, 'of Broadcasting House or the House of Commons?' To which McCulloch Jnr quipped, 'Well . . . No. But I did talk to Mr King about selling Tower Bridge and he said he didn't want to do that.'

And that in a sense is that.

It is again possible that McCulloch Jnr was simply putting an extraordinarily brave face on a monumental error. But by this stage granite had been inspected, contracts signed, blueprints drawn up, architects and civil engineers employed, shipping companies hired and London Bridge – not Putney, Westminster, Waterloo, Southwark, Hammersmith, Hungerford, nor Chelsea and definitely not Tower Bridge – was going to Lake Havasu City, Arizona, USA.

But perhaps naturally enough, Woody, McCulloch and Robert Jnr couldn't resist hankering after its rather more famous-looking neighbour – a Disneyland Magic Castle of a bridge if ever there

was one. And McCulloch Jnr's gauche, off-the-cuff admission of
that, is just the kind of comment that, come that lunchtime pint in
the Hat and Feathers, has already been transformed into: 'Americans,
eh? Those idiots are only going to put London Bridge up on dry
land. And, you know what, they really wanted Tower Bridge, I
heard it on the radio this morning.' And so the Chinese whispers
have gone on ever since, their legitimacy only bolstered by a
plethora of further tales about a sly British con artist who took
many all-too-innocent Americans abroad for a monumental ride.

CHAPTER 11

A Transatlantic Crossing

In June 1968, the sale of London Bridge was commemorated with the release of an updated pop version of the classic nursery rhyme by the Spectrum. Apparently fashioned (or later refashioned) by RCA Records as a British take on the Monkees, this heavily promoted five-piece could almost be viewed as an English attempt to copy an American copy of the Beatles, a band whose early repertoire itself owed a substantial debt to the R&B 78s carried across the Atlantic to Liverpool by US sailors. But despite mining such a previously winning transatlantic formula, their cannily timed single 'London Bridge is Coming Down' failed to chart. The record offers an endearingly jaunty reflection on the landmark's fate from the period. To the accompaniment of a wheezy organ, fuzzy electric guitar, a fret-scampering bass line and an almost reggae-ish offbeat, the song muses on the untrammelled march of progress and its role in the bridge's imminent departure via ship and lorry from the Surrey Docks to Lake Havasu City – a place Rennie's span, they are sure, will only help to make look pretty and mighty.*

---

* This was not to be the only musical response to the sale. Melodic rockers Bread provided 'London Bridge', a rather more downbeat, if not to say maudlin, account of the landmark's departure from the capital on their eponymous debut LP in 1969. And a year later, Jimmy Webb, the American

Along with putting out headline-snaffling novelty singles, the Spectrum's other claim to fame was performing the theme tune to the marionette science-fiction TV show *Captain Scarlet*, its creators Gerry and Sylvia Anderson having signed the band up as a kind of spin-off pop outfit for the programme. For press photographs they donned the same colour-coded militaristic uniforms designed by Sylvia for the puppets in the series, and starred in their own cartoon adventure strip in *Lady Penelope*, a weekly comic named after the Sloaney lead female character in *Thunderbirds* and aimed at the gymslip-wearing fans of the Andersons' output. In their initial appearances in the comic, the group were portrayed running an antique shop on the Portobello Road in between musical engage-ments. (Samuel Smiles' ethos of self-sufficiency and hard graft, it appeared, was alive and well in this *Eagle* for girls.) The reason for this dual identity (pop stars by night, peddlers of bric-a-brac by day) was that the West London street market had been the subject of an earlier Spectrum single – a record that had carried them on to *Top of the Pops*, if (sadly again) not into the top forty. If mostly lauding the Portobello Road and judging its array of Georgian and Victorian wares far superior to those at the rival Chelsea antique fair, the song's writers, John Marsh and Andrew Veal, couldn't resist noting, eyebrows ever so slightly arched, that its stallholders were apt to be unbelievably friendly to visiting American customers.

And studiously glossing over the relative youthfulness of a large

---

tunesmith responsible for 'Up, Up and Away' and 'MacArthur Park', was to reference the bridge's move in his song 'P. F. Sloan'.

percentage of the available stonework – as any seasoned dealer working their pitch in Notting Hill would have undoubtedly done in a similar situation – London Bridge was classified as an antique for its American buyers. 'Officially', 1968 was its 137th birthday. As such, and under the same hundred-year ruling that had allowed Hearst to build up his vast store of European treasures, it was therefore exempt from US import duties. Either to enshrine that somewhat flaky 'antique' status or, more likely, merely to drum up added publicity, Ivan Luckin had telephoned his friend Norris McWhirter. A former athlete, sports journalist, litigious right-winger, megaphone-wielding chider of Aldermaston anti-nuclear marchers and fellow buddy of Denis Thatcher, McWhirter was the co-creator and editor, with his identical twin brother Ross, of *The Guinness Book of Records*. And after batting various possibilities back and forth, Luckin persuaded McWhirter to include the bridge deal in that year's book of records under the hitherto unknown, and decades since rescinded, category of 'The Sale of the World's Largest Antique'.*

Once the immediate furore over the sale had subsided, the Spectrum single remaindered in Woolworths and the world record filed away for inclusion in an annual that inevitably would remain unread by anyone other than trivia fanatics and the fanatical

---

* Culturally, antiques seem to have loomed large in 1968. That year Keith Waterhouse published *The Bucket Shop*, a novel revolving around a hapless, adulterous antique dealer in Fulham. While Tom Courtenay, previously the on-screen incarnation of Waterhouse's daydreaming anti-hero *Billy Liar*, also appeared in *Otley*, a comic spy caper about a Portobello Road trader mistaken for a secret agent.

brothers themselves, the business of transporting the 10,000 tons of the bridge's stone to Arizona got rapidly under way.

As the old bridge started to be taken apart, the sections singled out to be preserved were carted off to a special unit at the Surrey Docks ahead of shipping to the States. To ensure nothing went astray, Alan Saines, a lone seventeen-year-old apprentice, was tasked with hand-painting a code on to each two-to-five-ton block as they came down, indicating its original location and what it had been attached to.

Other pieces, which were to be used to face the underlying new concrete bridge in Lake Havasu, the skeleton the old bridge's stone would be fitted on to, had to be cut down to size at the Merivale Quarry in Devon. Like the Pilgrim Fathers who put into Bayard's Cove en route to the New World in 1620, these particular fragments of the bridge sailed from Dartmouth. From either the Surrey Dock or Dartmouth, the remains of the Rennies' London Bridge would then undergo a 10,000-mile journey down the Atlantic, through the Panama Canal and around the coast of Mexico, before reaching Long Beach, California. From there the stone was loaded on to trucks and driven the last 300 miles to a holding 'corral' at Lake Havasu City. The first shipment, containing segments of the pier footings and the gigantic end pedestals, arrived at Long Beach, with suspiciously emblematic timing, on 4 July 1968 aboard a Swedish freighter named the *Agne*.

Swedish shipping agents would come to play an even greater role in getting the bridge to America as work got under way. By the end of the first year around 3,000 tons of stone, about a third of the granite sold, had found its way across the Atlantic in chartered ships. But most of the stone, if trussed up for hauling aboard, was packed and shipped loose, with the result that a good many pieces were chipped or quite severely damaged in transit. A certain they-can-sort-it-out-at-their-end attitude also flourished in London, leaving the Americans with the added headache – despite the pieces having been painstakingly numbered by Master Saines – of sorting through disparate piles of masonry to find which sections they had actually been sent. Concerned by this and the length of time it was taking, McCulloch hired the Johnson Line to handle the rest of the shipping – presumably he calculated that it would be cheaper in the long run for him to swallow this added expense, as the sooner the bridge was up the sooner Havasu could start attracting arch-fanciers and Anglophiles.

The Swedish shipping firm was among the pioneers of the latest innovation in marine trade: containerisation. This vastly reduced the number of hands needed to load and unload cargo, and made it economically viable to use much larger ships. With the Swedes packing some fifteen tons of stone into each open-topped container, and providing McCulloch's engineers with advance lists of what was being shipped in each individual container, the whole process became noticeably more efficient. Johnson's involvement in this of all contracts, though, was an ominous portent of the wholesale closure of London's docks over the next twelve years – from a peak of over 30,000 in the 1950s, the number of London dockers would shrink to a mere 2,000 at the end of 1981.

The bridge's foundation stone was laid in a jolly ceremony by Sir Gilbert Inglefield, the lord mayor of London, accompanied by his retinue, all clad in their official get-up (gold chains, silk gowns, furs, ermine, pikestaffs and all) on a spot of parched ground on the eastern, or city, side of Lake Havasu on 23 September 1968.* However, before the rest of what was left of London Bridge could be put back together again, the hollow substructure comprised of 33,000 tons of steel-reinforced concrete had to be built first.

As Robert McCulloch Jnr had informed listeners to the *Today* programme, there are considerable advantages in constructing a bridge on dry land. Perhaps the greatest is that instead of building a huge wigwam of scaffolding in the middle of a river to construct the arches, you can just pile a mountain of earth up, put your arch together over it, and then remove the soil once the structure is secure. And at Lake Havasu, after the pier footings were accurately in position, five neatly shaped mounds of Mojave desert sand were subsequently amassed around them. On top of these vast undulating humps, the substructure – a grey concrete span, sprouting supporting metal rods and steel loops here and there – was gradually assembled by a crew of forty men over the course of a year.

All of this was supervised by Robert Beresford, a British engineer who had arrived in Lake Havasu with a portfolio of the City's blueprints, drawings and photographs of London Bridge and – just to add to the rumours – a miniature model of Tower Bridge. This model was to occupy pride of place on his desk, occasionally serving as a paperweight, as he and Carl Barker from McCulloch

* One waggish local erected a wooden sign on the arid site with the injunction 'No Fishing from the Bridge' painted on it.

Properties Inc. plotted every stage of the bridge's reassembly. Things progressed well. By late 1970, and under Beresford's guidance, a small team of stonemasons from Mexico and Yugoslavia had moved in to begin lagging this substructure with the appropriate segments of London Bridge granite – sections of which were pockmarked with shrapnel damage from the Second World War or etched with century-old graffiti, and nearly all of which was blackened by traces of soot from the grimy metropolis it had previously served.

The corbels – the nine and a half feet supporting brackets in Cornish granite – were among the first pieces of Old London Bridge to be incorporated into the new substructure. To hurry this process along, Beresford devised a special crane to lift each particular stone into its designated slot. Despite this, more than a few stones were plugged in upside down or in the wrong order. But a span that looked to all intents and purposes – and to all but the

most eagle-eyed and pedantic – the spit of London Bridge gradually began to assume shape under the unforgiving Arizona sun in
1971. What it had yet to do, of course, was cross any water.

To create the necessary mile-long channel through the peninsula
for that, a digger nicknamed 'the Ranger' was brought in from
Newport Beach, California. It would chew through over two million
cubic yards of the earth before the job was done. Then, following
a blast of dynamite, Lake Havasu's crystalline blue waters were
gently persuaded to assume their position under the bridge. The
contrast to the soiled brown of Old Father Thames, a waterway,
not unlike Steptoe Snr, that had grown fairly disgusting with age
– and if personified in the early 1970s would probably have had a
sixty-a-day Embassy Filter habit and drunk meths with a neat diesel
chaser – was marked. But motorboaters, generously filling the air
with the aroma of spent kerosene and dripping oil into the lake,
would soon help acclimatise the bridge to its new home – though
there was initially some concern about how the granite might fare
in such a dry climate after decades of being pounded by London
rain.

And in 1971, and in temperatures cresting 105 degrees, a deputation from that showery grey town, headed by the lord mayor of London, Sir Peter Studd, the City sheriff, Murray Fox, and Ivan Luckin (along with a flock of the British capital's pigeons imported for the occasion), had a chance to inspect the resurrected London Bridge in all its new solar-dazzled glory when they were invited to attend its official opening.

The ribbon-snipping ceremony on 9 October and the bridge's dedication the next day were preceded by weeks of festivities. Among the parades and parties was a historical-costume competition with a brace of Maid Marians, bosoms heaving in tightly laced bodices, a couple of truly perfect gentle knights armoured in aluminium foil, some stovepipe-hatted Puritans in starched white collars, a cowboy or two, and a smattering of ragged-trousered Dickensian chimney sweeps and Little Nells, doing their best to look pallid and wan in the heat, all assembling to receive $7,000-worth of prizes awarded by the visiting lord mayor.

By the afternoon of the opening, Lake Havasu looked like the circus had come to town. On the roadway of the bridge stood a vast configuration of red and white striped canvas awnings, rigged up by a specialist team from Los Angeles. The main tent prepared for the gala dinner alone stood close to forty feet high and pole to pole weighed nearly twenty tons. Once erected, three five-feet-wide mock-crystal chandeliers were hoisted up into its canopy and nearly every inch of the floor below was covered by seventy round tables, each orbited by ten gold and red chairs, themselves satellites to a centre-stage head table, 112 feet long. The walls of the tent were adorned with pendants, battle standards, coats of arms and shields. Empty suits of armour lined the entrance to the marquee and the overwhelming impression created was that Richard the Lionheart might possibly be returning from the Crusades. Only the flatware, refined wine glasses, coffee stations and humming refrigeration units and the glint off the optics and ice buckets in a neighbouring cocktail tent dented the illusion that the onlooker hadn't, like Mark Twain's Hank Morgan, been pitched back into that age of chivalry, lethal plagues, poor dental hygiene and anti-Semitic monarchs.

If the onset of darkness, rapid as a switch and here tripped sharply at 5.30 p.m., was eerily reminiscent of power cuts at home for the visiting Londoners, then a recording of the familiar chimes of Big Ben half an hour later was to signal the beginning of that evening's festivities. With the VIPs (the mayor, the governor of Arizona, McCulloch, Woody, Luckin and respective wives) already assembled at the head table, invited guests (locals and the great and the good) filed on to the bridge and into the tent to take their seats, entertained en route by a band of Pearly Kings and Queens belting out 'Knees Up Mother Brown' and a wandering troupe of madrigal singers supported by a juggler and a magician. A succession of starter dishes – miniature fried Monte Cristo sandwiches, Chinese egg rolls in an apricot sauce, Lobster Newburg, stuffed mushrooms, quiche Lorraine, teriyaki steak rounds, hot Louisiana spiced Alaskan king crab – whose calorie count would today probably do for breakfast, lunch and supper combined, were served. At around 7 p.m. a trumpet fanfare announced the arrival of a flotilla of torchlit boats on the channel. As the vessels cruised under the arches of London Bridge to cheers from crowds on the bank, those above set about 'opening' the bridge by investigating its roadway. Three-quarters of an hour later, another trumpet call was followed by a burst of fireworks, the pumpf, fizz, crackle and bang of rockets lighting up the sky. When that was over, a kilted piper coaxed the diners to resume their positions in the tent, where Lorne Greene, the snow-haired mainstay of the TV Western *Bonanza*, addressed them.

Acting as master of ceremonies, Greene, once billed as 'the Voice of Canada' by his native national radio station, introduced the lord mayor, the governor, McCulloch and Woody et al. with the same sonorous gravitas as he frequently utilised to dispense sage advice to misguided horse rustlers at Ponderosa Ranch, or deployed in recounting the life and death of the famous Arizona outlaw Johnny 'Ringo' Peters on his unlikely 1964 Billboard chart-topping single – its meteoric success seemingly unconnected to the popularity of a certain band of loveable British mop tops at that time. The formalities and speeches over, a main course of belt-loosening proportions was dished up. Among the morsels on offer were half a guacamole-dressed lobster per diner, Cornish pasties, sirloin steaks, cannelloni Florentine and champagne-glazed baby carrots. Wine flowed until midnight, when another more spectacular firework display – 'the largest ever held in Arizona' – closed the opening.

The following morning, and in spite of a plethora of throbbing heads around town, there was still time for a sunrise service on the banks of the Bridgewater, the channel running now under the bridge, and a parachuting display before the dignitaries reconvened for the formal dedication. At around 10.30 a.m. and emulating William IV's journey along the Thames in 1831, the lord mayor Sir Peter Studd boarded a miniature paddle steamer at the Nautical Inn to taxi down to the bridge. (This steamer was called *Miller's Folly* and true to its name sank some years later.) Honouring the occasion, Studd wore his full ceremonial garb and making no concessions to the Arizona weather, he stepped on to the boat in a silver-buttoned tailcoat, gold-trimmed black silk robes, a lace-collared shirt, knee-length breeches; the whole ensemble finished off with a plumed tricorn and his bulky chain of office with its diamond-encrusted coat of arms. Accompanying him, and no more sensibly dressed, were the men at arms: Brigadier Robert Home Stewart Popham, in a Russian sable cap and carrying his sword, and St John Carslake Brooke-Johnson with the mace; and bringing up the rear were the high sheriff of London, Murray Fox, done up in scarlet, his deputy, Leslie Prince, in violet, and a company of twelve pikemen and musketeers.

Again Lorne Greene was on hand for the introductions, as McCulloch, Woody, the state governor and the rest of the bigwigs were dropped off at a special platform at the end of the bridge by a fleet of limousines – the actor's echoey amplified voice floating out above the percussive sounds of the attendant

University of Arizona marching band. Once the mayor and his retinue had disembarked from the steamer to Bridgewater bank side, and exchanged greetings with the governor, a nineteen-gun salute was fired and the band broke into 'God Save the Queen', promptly seconded by 'The Star-Spangled Banner'.

Turning to speak to the crowd, the lord mayor expressed his belief that the transplanted bridge would serve as 'a lasting monument' to 'the bonds of friendship and mutual goodwill . . . between the American and British people'. The fine words over, the governor and the mayor stepped forward to jointly pull a cord to release a hot-air balloon. Styled after the one Mr Green the Aviator had used to hover over events in 1831, as it rose, the balloon pulled away a red piece of drapery revealing the commemorative plaque.

Something akin to a cross between a Fourth of July parade and an episode of the game show *It's a Knockout* then ensued until sunset. Chemehuevi Indians in full battle dress and Boy Scouts holding flags for each of the fifty states headed up a mile-long crocodile of floats presenting a mobile historical tableau of London Bridge's life and times, peopled by Roman centurions, horn-helmeted Vikings and medieval monks. Penny-farthing bicyclists, cockney costermongers, baton-twirling majorettes and 'Beefeater' Yeomen of the Guard appeared. Jousting, archery, waterskiing and sky-kiting contests were held. Olde Tyme music-hall numbers and Broadway show tunes were sung. And at the expansive Odessa Chuck Wagon Gang barbecue pit, Eliza

Doolittle-esque cockney sparrows, Arthurian knights and Mojave County law officers could be spied hungrily tucking into plates of ribs, side by side.

At dusk, another Western star of the screen, Dale Evans Rogers, third wife and musical partner of the singing cowboy Roy, came out to lead a religious service (it was a Sunday, and she an evangelical), and the whole spectacle ended in prayer.

Although the Londoners would soon be taking their leave of Arizona, packing up their breeches, pikestaffs and tricorns and leaving London Bridge (or bits of it) behind them, a small part of Lake Havasu would now officially belong to the City of London.

It appears that this rather peculiar land deal was brokered during the laying of the foundation stone in October 1968, and largely because McCulloch and Woody, unusually for such a pair of consummate operators, were caught on the hoof that day. Sir Peter Studd, then a mere alderman sheriff and a few months away from his ennobling, was among the London party at that ceremony too. Part of his job had been to dispense various tokens of goodwill from the City to the Americans – crystal bowls and bottles of brackish Thames water, you name it. But this act took McCulloch and Woody completely by surprise. It hadn't occurred to them to bring gifts. The Brits had naturally been flown out to Lake Havasu gratis in one of McCulloch's Lockheed planes, they were being personally chauffeured around in one of the company's forty white Jeep Wagoneers, and wined, dined and given the best suites the Nautical Inn had to offer. But then there had been that slightly embarrassing incident over the reservations. All those titles were enough to confuse anyone. And they were from Europe . . . the girl at the front desk had seen *Jules et Jim*. Tallying up the kingsize double room booked for Mr Alderman, Mr Sheriff and Mrs Studd with the middle-aged couple in front of her, she'd just asked when Mr Alderman would be joining them. It was a mistake anyone could have made. And now, there was this. Sir Gilbert Inglefield and Alderman Sheriff Studd and their entourage were approaching with what looked like armfuls of gifts. McCulloch and Woody could only stare at their empty hands with a quickening dread. This was going to be embarrassing. What could they do? Fleet-footed in his saddle shoes, McCulloch had a brainwave. Why not give them a plot of land? If Lake Havasu could have London Bridge, why couldn't London have a piece of Lake Havasu? And that is what they did.

Mockingly referred to as 'an acre of dirt' by the locals, the plot was transferred over to the Corporation of London via the registration of an American company, The City of London (Arizona Corporation), established to administer its upkeep and run its facilities as a moneymaking tourist venture. This company's directors were to be entirely composed of aldermen and members of the Common Council of the City of London. Luckin was a lifelong member of its board – and interest in the company (and Lake Havasu) seems to have waned sharply after his death. However, on the completion of the bridge, this 'acre of dirt' was developed into a themed English village beside the Bridgewater Channel. Replete with a red Gilbert Scott telephone box, a stone fountain surrounded by lions modelled after Landseer's at Trafalgar Square (if made on the cheap in Mexico) and a row of gift shops in the Tudorbethan vein with gnarly roofs and crooked beams selling cockney wares, sunglasses and fishing gear, the village also had a 'real' English pub, the Hog in Armour, and, next door, an English restaurant, the City of London Arms, serving traditional British food – the roasts, fish and chips, steak and kidney pies and chips, mushy peas, chips and more chips, that did so much to enhance the nation's culinary reputation after the war. Later an old red London bus converted into an ice-cream parlour was added to the village's 'authentic' attractions.

Over in London, meanwhile, some were starting to feel that such traditional features were becoming increasingly rare in their own city.

Within months of London Bridge opening in Arizona, the market at Covent Garden, a purveyor of fruit and vegetables since the days when Nell Gwynn was squeezing King Charles II's oranges (or, if you prefer, was his orange-selling squeeze), was moved out to Nine Elms and the GLC finalised plans to demolish its Piazza buildings. Queenhithe, the last of the City of London docks, had already gone, bulldozed in less than a month to make room for a new hotel. Maple's on Tottenham Court Road, once proudly able to boast that it was 'the Largest Furniture Store in the World', closed its doors. As did Gamage's emporium in Holborn, redeveloped out of existence after ninety-four years of brightening childhood Christmases with its annual bazaar and floor-spanning model railway.

And much as the Westway, a concrete megalosaurus 'wading like an elephantine lizard' through the streets of North Kensington and Paddington, was to impose itself on the landscape, opening in 1970, the new London Bridge too arose, unloved but grudgingly accepted as an infrastructural necessity. The first arch on the Southwark bank and the so-called 'Nancy steps'* were preserved *in situ*. But the pre-stressed concrete replacement bridge that was laid on top of them seemed entirely, almost belligerently, indifferent to history. With foot-wide stainless-steel handrails resting on low parapets of polished granite, at road level it had all the allure of a motorway hard shoulder. Here was a bridge that possibly only characters in a J. G. Ballard novel could form a romantic attachment to.

---

* These are named after their walk-on part in Dickens' *Oliver Twist* – Bill Sikes' honest-hearted moll Nancy has her fateful meeting with Mr Brownlow and Rose Maylie on the (then brand new) London Bridge, the Rennie crossing serving as a link between criminal and civic society in the novel.

In an article for the *Guardian* entitled 'London Bridge is Up Again' and published on Friday 16 March 1973, the day of its official opening, William Holford, the man who supplied the new bridge's 'architectural treatment', invited the public to commend 'an exercise in the insertion of a new muscular structure into an ancient setting'. Elsewhere in the piece, Holford reiterated his vision of an altitudinal London dominated by firmament-scratching pedestrian decks. 'In twenty years' time', he predicted, 'the high-level walkways in the city may reach London Bridge and it will then be feasible to link them with a central corridor, glazed and roofed and supported by columns springing from the central dividing strip on which the existing street lights stand.' If the pedestrian traffic was sufficient, he saw no reason why 'two-way moving pavements' couldn't be built ' sixteen feet above the existing carriageway' allowing commuters to 'read a newspaper as they were being conveyed to and fro across London Bridge'.

Fearing a potential IRA bomb attack – and concerns about the Queen's safety were running especially high, as earlier in that same week Prince Philip, on a state visit to Australia, had his tour of Sydney disrupted by the discovery of a nail bomb on his official route – and unwilling to countenance a major disruption to traffic, with a strike by railway workers in full swing and another by the miners in the offing, the new bridge's 'opening' ceremony was a substantially more subdued affair than its predecessor had enjoyed either in 1831 or in Arizona, only eighteen months earlier. Still, a crowd of some 8,000 people assembled to witness the Queen open the latest Thames crossing. While that was slightly more than had

attended the Lake Havasu festivities, as a percentage of their respective populations and visiting sightseers, it added up to a poor showing for the British capital. The bridge, completed in the autumn of 1972, and fully operational for some months already, had to be closed to motor vehicles for the duration of the ceremony.

On the morning of the opening itself, police patrols were out in force and anyone venturing near London Bridge had their bags searched. Treated to as frosty a reception as Robert Peel in 1831, the Tory prime minister Edward Heath, at loggerheads with the trade unions and presiding over an economy on the skids, was booed upon his arrival.* But the Queen, protected by uniformed and plain-clothed officers as well as the pikemen and musketeers of the Honourable Artillery Company (described by the *Guardian* as looking 'like tubby counterparts of the Pope's Swiss Guard') met only cheers when she loomed into sight on the ML (motor launch) *Nore* from Westminster Pier. Greeted by the new lord mayor, Lord Mais, as she disembarked at the steps of the Fishmongers' Hall by the side of the bridge – a building that dated from the Rennie bridge redevelopments in 1831 – the Queen was hailed by the guns of the Tower of London battery. Escorted along the downstream carriageway to the centre dais, where she unveiled a plaque and declared the bridge open, the Queen undertook her signature

---

* Shortly before this, Bernard Levin in *The Times* wondered if Edward Heath had 'any idea what a man earning £20 a week feels when he sees speculators about to make untold millions by befouling Piccadilly Circus and Covent Garden and indeed any other bits of any other city they can get their hands on?'

walkabout among the crowds and was photographed chatting to a schoolboy in an askew cap seemingly lifted straight out of the pages of Richmal Crompton's *Just William*. These pleasantries over with in a couple of hours, she left and normal service was resumed, with only the backfiring of Austin Maxis offering any further pyrotechnical salutes that day. Within nine months of the opening, this meagre tribute to a bridge specifically designed to increase London traffic flow by accommodating 40,000 cars appeared even more laughable. The OPEC oil crisis coupled with the miners' strike rendered fuel so scarce that Ted Heath's government was forced to introduce petrol rationing, leaving many motorists with little option but to abandon their cars. Concerned that it could undermine public morale, Heath intervened to prevent the Queen from alluding to the unravelling crisis in that year's Christmas Speech.

PART THREE

We Were Somewhere Around Barstow: Lake Havasu City, Arizona, 2011

I knew it was in the desert but I never expected it to be quite so deserted. Absence is, of course, the essential characteristic of a desert landscape. And it is the substantial lack of greenery, houses, inhabitants, any features really, other than bare red rock, eroded sediment and loamy fine sand that lends the Mojave a monotonous kind of beauty. What vegetation there is out there – creosote bush, bursage, Cat Claw, mesquite, names that could double up as brands of bourbon or beer – pokes out of the stony ground like bristles on a hog. Only the Joshua trees, their branches contorting as if dancing or wrestling, offer some relief from the almost oppressive barrenness of this terrain. Entering the limits of Lake Havasu City, palm trees, imported at the city's birth, do their utmost to gild a topography that remains close to lunar in its aridity. Large cinder block buildings and low-slung ranch houses sit in lonely expanses of rocky ground. They could almost be space stations on some crater of Mars. And the prevalence of motorboats on trailers, lined up in dry, powdery yards, only adds to the unearthliness of it all, by conveying the impression that an ocean must have recently boiled away. A lead item in the local newspaper, the *Today's*

News-Herald, picked up at the gas station, is headlined 'Wild pig invaders must go'. The lake when it finally comes into view, pellucid and a shimmery greeny blue, looks unsurprisingly like a mirage.

And London Bridge? It seems almost curiously right. Under a blazing sun and a pure cerulean sky, its reconstructed neoclassical arches appear strikingly refined over the glistening channel, and far more convincingly Greco-Roman than they (surely) could ever have done in London. Freed from the confines of an exceedingly snug cityscape boasting a distracting array of architectural sights, the Rennies' bridge is able to assume centre stage here, like a much passed-over Hollywood star finally enjoying a second wind as a lead in a TV soap.

However, the English Village, its channel-side brother in arms, is not wearing nearly so well. Though the visitor enters the 'village' through a pair of imposing crested iron gates – another import from

England, though Gloucestershire rather than the Guildhall – and comes face to face with a silver City of London griffin, the City itself relinquished its interest in the 'acre of dirt' over two decades ago. Its various concessions and shops, technically managed from London but obviously staffed on the ground by locals, were, apparently, simply a gift to till skimmers in a pre-Internet, pre-EPOS age, and the City came to deem the whole enterprise as more trouble than it was worth. Beyond the griffin, there is a small town square, dominated by a central fountain guarded by 'fun-sized' replicas of Landseer's Nelson's Column lions and edged by the Visitor Center, a wooden clocktower, a mock mock-Tudor pub and a Gilbert Scott telephone box. But the red telephone box is now missing a door – and a telephone. And the pub, the London Arms (formerly the Hog in Armour), has shut down and is boarded up. A red London bus that also once stood here has long been banished to a distant repair yard, and stripped of its engine. Moving off from the square into a narrow street of half-timbered stores and booths and kiosks, all but one were closed and empty. It was late September and, admittedly, out of season. But the blistered paint, nailed doors and grimy windows all indicated that this was a far from recent, and rather more permanent, state of affairs. The whiff of decay was unavoidable, and one reminiscent of clapped-out seaside resorts, amusement parks and holiday camps the world over. And only the occasional jogger, and a handful of visitors, ever seemed to venture along its empty high street in the time I was there, with the latter mostly scurrying back to the bridge and the waterfront as if embarrassed to have made a wrong turn.

Still, the English Village is only a fraction of Lake Havasu, and this new town, this new city (not actually incorporated until 1988), that had a population of just 4,000 residents when London Bridge was purchased in 1968, and had quadrupled within a decade of its opening, today is home to around 53,000 – roughly around the same as Margate in Kent after 200 years as a coastal resort. That figure remains a smidgen over half the 90,000 McCulloch envisioned but it represents for a settlement of its ilk and age a success. And those numbers are bolstered every winter by the arrival of the 'snow birds' – retirees and seasonal drifters who flock here, usually in their RVs, from Wyoming, Wisconsin, Minnesota, Idaho, Missouri, Utah and Colorado to avoid the cold – and each spring 'break' by college students, who for the last twenty years or so have established a reputation for going extremely 'wet and wild' on the lake. Pasties – those miniature fez hats for nipples – are heavily advertised on the boards outside the shops at the London Bridge Resort. Situated on the eastern side of the bridge to the English Village, it's a parallel complex concentrated around a large hotel whose main lobby is dominated by a replica of Elizabeth II's coronation coach. ('The only one in the world,' the hotel receptionist informed me, cheerily. Quickly adding, 'Other than the original, obviously.') Its emporiums and amusements are also shut for the most part. But it is in noticeably better shape than its overtly faux British neighbour. And although some economic casualties are visible, its numerous closures appear more obviously a barometer of seasonal requirements rather than long-term failure per se.

According to Doug Traub, Lake Havasu's ebullient Convention and Visitors' Bureau president, in a 2010 survey of Lake Havasu's most popular attractions, London Bridge – *the* bridge – came in *tenth* place. If for the English visitor* that initially seems a relatively, if not to say depressingly, modest ranking, it's worth noting that the span, however attractive, was up against 116 other options in this survey, including four golf courses. 'About thirty per cent of the people who visited in the last twelve months', Traub explained over the telephone, 'visit the bridge specifically, whereas forty per cent will come here just to sunbathe. The most popular thing is the lake itself, fifty-eight per cent of people come here to go to the lake. So the bridge is about half as popular as the lake itself. The most-liked features of Lake Havasu are its natural beauty, the friendly people, the laid-back atmosphere – and the lake.' But,

* Okay, *this* English visitor.

he maintained, when visitors were asked to choose one of ten captions that best described Lake Havasu City – ranging, apparently, from the somewhat immodest 'Jet Ski Capital of the World' to 'Most Patriotic City in America' – 'Home of London Bridge' was the clear winner. And in another survey, 'The bridge comes out as the second "most visited attraction" in the state behind the Grand Canyon. And this year we will top 93,000 visitors, and we've stepped up the offering for folks with a new brochure, and we're introducing a walking tour to London Bridge, so it remains an important element of the identity of our city.'

* * *

'You know it's hollow, right?' Jan Kassies asked, the question accompanied by a thumb motioned hitchhiker-style in the direction of London Bridge and addressed to myself and two correspondents from *American Iron*, a magazine for Harley Davidson enthusiasts. The biker journalists had swung by Lake Havasu on a whim en route to a rally in Las Vegas, and constituted the only other members of that day's guided tour. It was 11 a.m., already approaching 90 degrees, and all three of us clutched paper beakers of hot coffee, much as seasick passengers on a boat might grip a rail for support. Registering the bikers' genuine astonishment, Kassies continued, 'Oh yes, bats live inside it,' breaking into a slight chuckle as he imparted, with obvious relish, this rather Gothic piece of information. 'You can see them flutter in and out at night.'

A nimble, almost impish, sixtysomething with snowy hair and a peppery grey-white goatee beard, twinkly blue eyes and a Dutch accent, Kassies has the slightly otherworldly demeanour of a sage in a science-fiction fantasy movie – the type of elder figure who invariably crops up to tutor the impetuous male lead in some arcane religion and combat with laser weaponry.

His own trajectory from Europe in some ways mirrors that of the bridge he was to spend an hour diligently escorting us around, directing our attention, in particular, to numerous upside-down bricks and a piece of graffiti left by an American serviceman stationed in London during the Second World War – and dismissing a question on the Tower Bridge myth, with the no-nonsense response, 'Oh that was McCulloch. He made that up. He was a jokester, just to get media attention.'

From the east of Holland, and a teacher in Hardenberg for many years, Kassies took early retirement in his late fifties, sold up and moved to Columbus, Ohio, after meeting and falling in love with an American woman. A year after that she too retired and the couple settled in Lake Havasu. But instead of kicking back by the lake, Kassies began volunteering at the tourist Visitor Center and was soon enough coaxed out of retirement completely to become its full-time director. 'I wasn't expecting to work again and I do forty hours most weeks now. Maybe,' he quipped, 'I will do it till I fall down, or the bridge does.' Neither looks likely any time soon. Although if the city's burghers get their way, within the next decade London Bridge will be joined by a new and 'extremely futuristic' bridge alongside it to ease the traffic flow. 'In the old days, when they'd first built the city, they'd just close the bridge off and put tents on it and have a party. But now we have lots of people living on the island, we have hotels and people have to come and go, so you can't ever close the bridge off. We are still a pretty small town, and if there are four or five cars in a row we call it a traffic jam here.'

This, it emerged, was far from the only plan afoot in Lake Havasu City. A scheme to demolish the remnants of the English Village, replacing it with a marina, a shopping complex, parking facilities, and a series of high-end condos was being voted on that very week. The proposals, eventually passed with a clear majority, had been extremely contentious. The fiercest debate was generated by the design itself whose principal motif was a trio of eight-storey towers on the waterfront. But some older residents expressed alarm that a piece of Lake Havasu City history – of which there was precious little to start with – was to be swept aside.

Kassies, although a relative newcomer, seemed sanguine about the change. 'I think the English theme was getting a little old, a bit tired; it wasn't working any more. It had failed. The firm running it foreclosed. Some people are sad to see it go, yes. Some would like it not to change and feel that the place has gotten too big already. But we have a chance to build something better – I hope it will be better, anyway – it will be a nice modern spot to boat and shop, with a wonderful walkway and seating areas, and London Bridge that will always be here.'

Each year, the arrival of the bridge continues to be celebrated in a run of parades, dinners, sporting contests and a rededication. And pulling out all the stops for the fortieth anniversary that October, the bridge was to be decorated with gruesome replicas, all bulgy-rubber eyes on stalks and lathered in fake blood, of the impaled heads of such traitors as William Wallace, Thomas More and revolting peasant Jack Cade. (An invitation was extended to the Duke and Duchess of Cambridge, but William and Kate regretfully declined.)

But according to Kassies, the highlight of the season for many is the annual lighting up of Cup Cake Mountain – a tradition that in part looks back to the 1920s. It was then that army troops stationed in the region noticed that a rare snowfall had left a frosted finish on the top of one of the mountains on the Whipple range on the Californian side of the Colorado River. Accordingly, they decided to christen it Cup Cake Mountain. And since it is the bridge's birthday, the crown of this mountain is circled with lights to resemble a Brobdingnagian birthday cake. If cherished by long-term inhabitants, this ritual creates havoc for the local police force, who are inundated with calls from visitors and new residents reporting sightings of unidentified flying objects. 'We assume it's Cup Cake Mountain but it *could be* UFOs,' Kassies suggested with admirably philosophical reasoning and not a trace of irony. 'You see a lot of strange lights here. I've seen a UFO myself, once. It was on a boat on Copper Canyon. I don't believe it was an alien but there were these four lights that moved in the same direction above us. It was very weird.' Later he would show us a photograph on his computer of a blurry apparition spotted in the window of the defunct waterfront clothing store LA Style. 'Some people tell me it looks like Jesus, but playing an organ,' he explained, pointing out a fuzzy pixelated smear on the monitor screen. 'It could be a ghost, but I don't know, there's definitely something odd there.'

These are not the only strange sightings in Lake Havasu. In the days immediately after the bridge opened in 1971, the shadowy figure of a woman in a long Victorian black dress was reputedly seen walking over the bridge. Press articles from the period wondered, though never especially seriously, if this might be the transplanted ghost of a jilted Miss Havisham-esque bride who had committed suicide, or a murdered cockney prostitute whose body was dumped in the Thames.*

Having crossed over to the island end of the bridge, where there is a life-sized statue of McCulloch and Woody in silvery bronze unfurling the plans for the City, similarly morbid, if not exactly paranormal, speculations came to mind. On reflection, it is almost odd that no one has ever reported catching a glimpse of a pale form in saddle shoes floating about the place after midnight. For Robert Paxton McCulloch's demise was most probably unpleasant, the precise details remain contested and murky and there was/is, arguably, plenty for a malevolent spectre to want to avenge. What is not in dispute is that he died aged sixty-five on 25 February 1977 and that around a hundred sleeping tablets, between ten and fifty codeine pills, and a substantial quantity of alcohol were sloshing around his system at the end. The Los Angeles County Coroner concluded it was an accident, which seems an assessment worthy possibly of Dario Fo.

Just three days before his death, McCulloch Properties Inc., a subsidiary of the McCulloch Oil Corporation, and in the words of the *New York Times* 'a major land-developer in Colorado and Arizona', pleaded guilty in a Denver Court to '19 misdemeanor counts of criminal fraud in connection with sales of its 27,000-acre

---

* If these stories appear eerily similar to the conceit of René Clair's 1935 film *The Ghost Goes West* – a Scots-ified adaptation of Eric Keown's *Sir Tristram Goes West*, a comic yarn about an English ghost who is accidentally shipped to America in a transplanted castle – their popularity also paved the way for David Hasselhoff to do battle with a spooky Jack the Ripper in Lake Havasu in the 1985 TV horror movie *Terror at London* (aka *Bridge Across Time*).

Pueblo West subdivision'. The firm's president, Robert McCulloch Jnr, agreed with the Pueblo Colorado District Attorney to pay 'about $16 million in money and land . . . to the district for improvements and water lines, roads, sewers and other facilities'. It was then the largest settlement in the state of Colorado's history and a damning indictment of sharp practice in the company's land-development wing. As many as a hundred salesmen were reportedly hawking tracts at one point and several were found to have made grossly inaccurate claims about the sites they were selling.

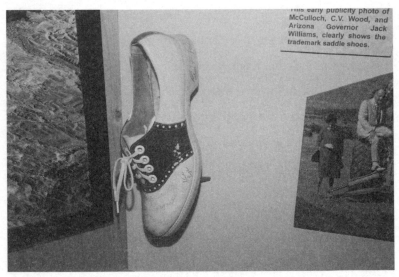

This early publicity photo of McCulloch, C.V. Wood, and Arizona Governor Jack Williams, clearly shows the trademark saddle shoes.

Around Lake Havasu City, however, old-timers continue to speak warmly of McCulloch Snr, recalling in particular the honesty with which he conducted his business here. Go to the local museum, for instance, housed in an unassuming lot about half a mile north of the bridge, where each stage of the area's history – from the discovery of the Colorado by Spanish conquistadors to the filming on the lake of the movie *Piranha 3D* – is lovingly charted with the aid of maps, models, films, photographs and period artefacts (McCulloch chainsaws and a signed saddle shoe among them). Here two of the city's earliest residents are regularly to be found staffing the front desk.

Lyle and Stellene Matzdorff have been in Lake Havasu longer than virtually anyone else. Lyle, today neat in a Hawaian shirt and cowboy jeans, was originally from the rather more verdant Iowa and opened the first real-estate office in the city in December 1963 – a month before McCulloch and Woody launched their fly-before-you-buy selling operation. Though 'city' is not strictly accurate since, as he explained, speaking slowly and very precisely throughout, there really 'wasn't anything here: nothing'. His office was a mobile home. One that he, his wife Stellene, and their ten-month-old son also lived in. But they considered themselves reasonably fortunate, as almost everyone else was still in tents then. 'It was tough,' Lyle said, touching the large silver frames of his glasses to emphasise the point. 'There was one telephone, over at Site Six. We'd queue up to use it. The nearest store until about the fall of that first year was a sixty-mile drive out to Kingman or Needles and back. If you were going, everyone would give you a shopping list, the women would organise a grocery pool.'

Despite the obvious hardships, Lyle enthused about the camaraderie and spirit of those early days and is justifiably proud of what they achieved. 'We did feel like pioneers. I was twenty-seven, and we had lots of young people, very healthy and strong. Young people built this town.' McCulloch, he maintained, however, was the one who ultimately made it work. 'He had a good sense of what would make a community. McCulloch was smart enough to say you can sell all the lots you like but that does not make a town. It takes people to do that. And he knew that if those people weren't happy they would soon give up, and, say "Hey, I wanna move back to LA or Phoenix, they've got stores down there!" And they really did go through the phone book and try to work out what we'd need here, getting guys from outside in, to open a garage and an appliance store, and building a bowling alley themselves because that was what every other town had. One time, when there weren't enough eggs in the store for an Easter hunt for the kids, McCulloch had his people fly some over in a D18 plane. He gave real attention to detail, and we could always count on him to help.'

In this period, he argued, even McCulloch's method of selling residential lots for families imbued Lake Havasu with a certain civic quality, absent in some other developments. 'You have to remember this was the 1960s, there were hundreds of land scams going on, people who sold land out in the middle of the desert, swamp land, crappy stuff. With McCulloch, you had to go and see it, book a flight, take a look and see if you liked it. That established a kind of trust between you and the company, and that trust was important, because right at the beginning all you were looking at was a promise. I mean all you could see was a proposed site for a shopping centre, a proposed site for a church, because nothing was there yet. But I think people responded to the idea of a new community here, and that community spirit got us through the early years, which were hard.'

Just how hard, and especially for the women, is emphasised by Stellene, who although demurely attired in a bright flowery summer dress, is given to rolling her eyes at some of Lyle's statements and interjecting with often far less rosy recollections of those early years. 'It was a man's town. It was all about fishing and boating – there was only one store. I used to have to drive to Needles for a laundromat to do the diapers. There were a lot of divorces, because the women didn't like it or couldn't cope. It was a huge culture shock. I'd lived in LA and Phoenix, we had a very nice house in Phoenix and every section corner had a shopping centre on it, and then,' she paused to glance in mock horror at her husband, 'we came here.'

'Real pretty cactus,' he retorted, with a wink, the quick-fire delivery implying the reprisal of an old comic routine, one honed to perfection over fifty years of marriage.

Before their double act could get into full Lucy and Desi swing, however, another pioneer, Neil Essene, a seventy-something in a sta-prest shirt and high-waisted shorts with a whip of snowy white hair, dropped in. 'I came here in '67, before the bridge. I was born and raised in Montana but then I lived in Kansas City for about eighteen years. I was working for a contractor and things were going to pot, our oldest was gonna start high school, the youngest junior high, and we wanted to get them out of the city. My wife and I came out here in March, I think. Everything in Kansas was dull, black and freezing, and we flew here. We arrived at about nine o' clock at night, and the water . . . It was like drinking water, it was just beautiful. That's what sold us.'

News that McCulloch had bought London Bridge, all three said, was greeted with astonishment in Lake Havasu at the time. 'We thought it was a joke,' Essene confessed. Stellene confirmed that this had been her reaction too. 'I remember Lyle told me, "McCulloch's bought this English London Bridge," and I said, "Oh you gotta be kidding me." I couldn't believe it. I think we all felt that way.'

Lyle, if admitting to finding the idea equally baffling to start with, believed it was one of the shrewdest decisions McCulloch ever made. 'I think he was getting a few of his land contracts back and things were looking shaky for a while. But then he bought London Bridge, and people started saying, "This town is gonna make it, you don't buy London Bridge for nothing." Things did pick up after that.'

'I heard,' Essene added, 'that they paid for the bridge before they ever got it here, just in land sales. Land sold like hot cakes, once people knew the bridge was coming here.'

With shipping and construction, McCulloch would spend a grand total of $7,500,000 on the bridge. Lyle is sure the chainsaw king got a bargain. 'It's had a lot of good history, "London Bridge is Falling Down" and all that. It will be famous forever. Every time someone goes down the highway to Interstate 140, and they see a sign for London Bridge, that's gotta get their attention, hasn't it?'

Leaving aside land deals, he is convinced that along with putting Lake Havasu on the map, it did wonders for McCulloch's stock price and that the old man also recouped some of his costs with sales of spare granite. He isn't sure how much spare granite there was, but somewhat tellingly, over forty years on, genuine pieces of London Bridge can still be purchased in the museum's shop, for $1 a go.

It turned out that Essene, a carpenter by trade, had built the original pub in the English Village. And although saddened by its more recent fate, he and the Matzdorffs accepted the need for the village's redevelopment. 'None of it,' he stated (and he if anyone should know), 'was built to last forty years.' Its part in Lake Havasu's story would be acknowledged here, in their museum – itself a testament to the city's ability to adapt to changing circumstances.

Nevertheless, Essene expressed some concern about the stewardship of that history, now that the pioneers were growing increasingly elderly – though he accepted a gibe from Lyle that 'the alternative was surely worse'. The pioneers are not the only ones getting older in Lake Havasu, though. Where the city once attracted twenty-somethings with children, newer residents tend to be retirees, or older – possibly remarried – couples seeking a fresh start. And although both the Matzdorffs' and Essenes' offspring have stayed in the area, raising families of their own here, it was more common for younger Havasuvians to leave town for college and/or work. The orgies of spring break aside, Lake Havasu, to reverse Nicholas Mosley's adage about Oxford, has become a young place for old(er) people, as the generous number of disability parking bays at the local Walgreens perhaps attests.

Tourism, or leisure in its broader sense, is the only industry to speak of here – with interrelated offshoots such as construction, real estate and boatbuilding, all previously major growth areas, having stalled since the financial crisis in 2008. McCulloch's plants, ironically given their initial significance, were relatively early economic casualties, with the chainsaw factory closing after Black and Decker acquired the business in the 1970s. At the end of that decade McCulloch Jnr and Woody were ousted from the board of McCulloch Oil et al., when the Houston financier and hedge-fund pioneer Charles E. Hurwitz gained control of the company. At that juncture, a quietly spoken forty-year-old with a preference for dark conservative three-piece suits and keeping a low public profile, Hurwitz was practically the anti-McCulloch, and as obverse a figure to Woody as possible to imagine. Later reviled for his junk-bond-funded takeover of the Pacific Lumber Company and a scheme to harvest some of California's oldest virgin redwood trees, he exemplified a new breed of Wall Street whizz-kid who would storm corporate America in the Reagan era. His conglomerate, MAXXAM, however, once memorably described in the *New York Times* as 'the sort of stock that [right-wing US radio talk-show host] Rush Limbaugh would pick if he ever decided to run his own socially conscious mutual fund', retains substantial holdings in Lake Havasu City.

If, by contrast, McCulloch and Woody cut a rather more romantic dash, the city has spent the intervening decades living with some of their unfulfilled promises and mistakes. Although not all of the latter could be foreseen, and there are some who claim that if McCulloch had lived longer they would have been resolved earlier, a picture of a rather haphazard, in places cavalier, approach to certain basic utilities is hard to avoid. To this day, the city does not have street lights, and even traffic lights proved something of an afterthought. The popularity of the lake and the channel with motorboaters has brought consistent problems with overcrowding and, on occasions, quite toxic levels of air and water pollution. And the city's sewage system had to be completely overhauled after its aquifer was discovered to be leaking contaminated material into the lake in the 1990s. Though again, some of these problems are to a degree markers of its success.

As Stanley Usinowicz, the former editor of the local *Today's News-Herald* newspaper, explained over good coffee and even better pastries at the Wired café on McCulloch Blvd – Lake Havasu's classic American 'Main Street' of barbershops and offices for the Republican Party, for a resort town – public parks were another blind spot for the founders. Today wearing a baseball cap that could easily be imagined as a substitute for a subeditor's green eyeshade, Usinowicz is an earnest, urbane, hot-metal-and-ink newspaperman of the old school. A Vietnam veteran, and an Anglophile who happened to be staying with friends in London when news of the bridge sale broke, he moved to Lake Havasu to take up a job on the paper in 1985. 'Even when I got here there still wasn't a lot to do. There was no recreation for the kids other than the lake, no park system to speak of.' But growth, he suggested, had helped fill those gaps in Lake Havasu's civic amenities. As had some elements of the original plan, such as Woody's avoidance of a grid street layout and the sale of individual rather than tract lots, which he argued had allowed the town to develop more organically than other places of its type. 'You have to remember,' he stressed, 'we are still a young community, this is a great place to live, I've always been happy here, we have a good community, but politically as much as anything else, we are still evolving.'

Brilliantly acerbic about the visiting spring breakers' indifference to London Bridge – 'To them it's just something that's fun to go under on a boat, so they can blast their horns and hear the echo' – Usinowicz got quite misty-eyed when recalling the days here when a best bitter could be supped from your own tankard at the London Arms and pigeons, descended from the ones imported for the opening ceremony, still roosted on Lake Havasu's rooftops. But, having seen the town more than double in size, whatever 'emotional memory' the English Village had for him and some of 'the old-timers', there was, he believed, 'simply no going back to the quaint feel of that, however much we might wish to'.

On a large table over from us, a local mothers' group was holding a meeting, and as we spoke, stout men in checkered Western shirts and preppy-ish office workers in chinos popped in for takeouts, exchanging pleasantries with the counter staff, other diners and the patron, Eileen, an indomitable, glamorous fifty-something blonde in the Dolly Parton vein. Discussions about a forthcoming golf club

dinner dance and the health of mutual friends mingled with a news report, coming at a low volume from a television screen fixed to a wall. Bustling with everyday life, the diner, to someone like myself suckled on American indie movies in England, took on the feel of one of those Robert Altman ensemble films: in every direction a little story seeming to be playing itself out. And while I was there apologies for the boringness of my drive from Los Angeles along Route 95 were given, polite questions asked about the Royal Wedding and an opinion sought on the British reaction to Obama's recent decision to remove a statue of Winston Churchill from the Oval Office. After I took a photograph with my film camera, jokes were good-naturedly cracked about everything in Britain being an antique, and suggestions of other places to eat and drink in town came quick and fast. Following up one, that night I headed to the Desert Martini.

Something of a local institution, this uptown tavern has been serving thirsty Havasuvians its eponymous cocktail for twenty-five years now. And it was that brew I purposefully set out to sample inside its windowless railcar-shaped interiors, over a few frames of pool and even a round of darts. My expectations had been low, I have to admit. On paper, the Desert Martini sounded fairly unprepossessing, if not actually plain disgusting. It is comprised of twenty ounces of beer served in an almost grotesquely proportioned iced martini glass goblet, with an olive in it – extra olives can be added for ten cents a throw. But today with the temperature an earth-parching 97 outside, no drink could have tasted better, the saltiness of the olives combining perfectly with the chilled, hoppy beer to quench a thirst that I hadn't noticed until then. As goblets were raised in a toast to London Bridge, it was yet another reminder that sometimes seemingly the most absurd things work perfectly wonderfully when combined in the right places.

Acknowledgements

Thanks are first due to everyone at Jonathan Cape, but most of all my editor, Alex Bowler, who not only responded so warmly to the idea of a book about the sale of London Bridge to Arizona, but also proved tireless in turning the sprawling mass of words eventually delivered (late) into something at least verging on readable. I am completely indebted to the Society of Authors, The Authors' Foundation and Arts Council England, who provided me with the grants that allowed me to travel to Lake Havasu City and the financial support that made writing this book possible.

Further thanks are due to my agent, Nicola Barr, and the team at Greene and Heaton for their efforts on my behalf. I am equally immensely grateful to the staff at the London Metropolitan Archives in Clerkenwell, the Local History Library, Southwark, the British Library in St Pancras and in Colindale, the London Library in St James's and Stoke Newington Library, who provided the various records, books, newspapers and pamphlets that I pillaged to write this book. I'd like to add special notes of thanks to Carol Morgan, the archivist at the Institution of Civil Engineers, who unearthed many essential plans, pictures and journals, Archie Galloway, whose own memories of Ivan Luckin were invaluable and who also nudged me in the direction of several key pieces in the puzzle, and Gareth Williams, the man from Auntie, who helped locate one of the others. Extra extra special thanks go to the fine poet, translator, film-maker and mustache-wearer (US spelling) David Shook for being 'my native companion' on the road trip to Lake Havasu City and whose enthusiasm for the project and Desert Martinis at times surpassed even my own.

Also a glass raised to his wife, Sydneyann Shook, and Jack Martinez, Jennifer Fowler, Geoff Gossett, Brian Hewes and Boris Dralyuk and their pets, children and favourite noir writers, tiki bars, taco stalls, and nameless Pho restaurants for making me feel at home in Los Angeles. Cheers too to Ian Whitcomb for sharing his thoughts on England and America, champagne and George Formby songs in Altadena, and Geoff Nicholson for proffering fish and chips in Hollywood and an opinion or ten on the book in progress and on Anglo-American relations in general.

In Lake Havasu City, thanks to everyone for welcoming a curious stranger, but most of all to Doug Traub, Jan Kassies, Michelle Gardia at Lake Havasu City Convention & Visitors Bureau, Mike Riddle, the curator at the Lake Havasu Museum of History, and Lyle and Stellene Matzdorff, Neil Essene and Stan Usinowicz, for giving up their time to answer my countless questions and sharing their own stories about life in Lake Havasu with me. For some of the spice on C.V. Wood, a big thank you to Carol Hancock at the International Chili Society.

Nick Rennison kindly read an early draft of the book and

provided many useful suggestions and corrections. As did Alex Mayor, who also created my author website and assembled the Pembury Players to stage a dramatic interpretation of parts of the book. And now I must simply resort to a list of friends, colleagues, previously kindly commissioning editors, and souls who have been nice along the way, and seek forgiveness from anyone I have inadvertently forgotten, so thank you: Bob Stanley, Pete Wiggs, Martin Kelly, Sarah Cracknell, Paul Kelly, Debsey Wykes, Cathi Unsworth, Marc Glendening and all the Sohemians, Mark Mason, Mark Pilkington, Joe Kerr, Charles Holland, Richard Davies, Gareth Evans, David Secombe, Graham Swift, Ian Jack, Paul Baggaley, Kris Doyle, Sophie Jonathan, Andy Miller, Andrew Martin, Alice Maddicott, Konrad Fredericks, Mark Augustyn, Russell Kane, Simon Grant, Guy Sangster-Adams, Lauren Wright, Gail O' Hara, Richard Boon, Deborah Cohen, Steve Jelbert, Dan Carrier, Andrew Holgate, John Doran, Luke Turner, Frances Morgan, Chris Roberts, Declan Clarke, Rachel Bailey, Catherine Taylor, Katrina Dixon, Michael Knight, Simon Hughes, Hannah Connelly, John Noi, Dusty Miller, Liz Vater, Pete Brown, Louise Campbell, Ashley Biles, Karen Mcleod, Henry Jeffreys, Paula Byerly Croxon, Sarah Maguire, Deborah Bourne, Tom Boll, Charles Beckett, Julia Bird, Katherine Pierpoint, Jamie McKendrick, Martin Orwin, Bill Herbert, Clare Pollard, Jenny Lewis, Helen Gordon, Mike Smith, Tom Chivers, Sam Hawkins and Marie McPartin, Jeremy Worman, Tim Wells, Anna Goodall, Peter Ho, Jody Porter, Richard Thomas and John Williams, Dotun Adebayo, Simon Bendle, Antonia

Turnball, Gerry Hopkinson, Raz at the Betsy Trotwood, Eleanor Lowenthal and David Dawkins at Pages of Hackney, Hereward Corbett, Dan Thompson, Jeff Barrett and Robin Turner, Darren Hayman, John Jervis, Daniel Trilling, Robin the Fog and Katie Bilboa, John Boyne, Neil Taylor, Dickon Edwards, Christian Flamm, Paul Lawrence, Oliver Dearden, Jerome Weatherald, Ella-mai Robey, Clare Gogerty, Lisa Sykes, Andrew Dunn, Liz Flanagan and the Ladies at Arvon, Lumb Bank.

Which leaves space, just about, to once again thank my folks without whom . . . my in-laws and extended family over the pond, and my wife, Emily Bick, whose brilliant mind and astonishing beauty I am *still* fortunate enough to be blessed with every day.

ILLUSTRATION CREDITS

SOURCES

This book owes an enormous debt to numerous previous books charting the development of bridges, civil engineering, London, America and Lake Havasu City.

The sources and select bibliography below should hopefully give credit where credit is due and point those who want to know more in the right directions.

Introduction

For the stone-laying ceremony at Lake Havasu and the subsequent opening jamboree, and much else throughout the rest of the book concerning London Bridge's journey to America in general, see:

—*New City Old Bridge*, Roger A. Johnson (Lake Havasu Historical Society 1981)

—*London Bridge Miracle*, Roman Malach (Mojave County Board of Supervisors 1981)

—*The Man Who Bought the London Bridge*, Donald Judson Frost (Lake Havasu Genealogical Society 1987)

—*Bridge Across the Atlantic: The Story of John Rennie*, Wallace Reyburn (Harrap: London 1972)

—*London Bridge*, Peter Jackson (Historical Publications Ltd: London 1971)

—*Crossing the River: The History of London's Thames River Bridges from Richmond to the Tower*, Brain Cookson (Mainstream: London/ Edinburgh 2006)

—*Cross River Traffic: A History of London's Bridges*, Chris Roberts (Granta: London 2005)

Irma Kurtz's comments about London being 'less like an American city' than any she'd known appear in *Dear London: Notes from the Big City* (Fourth Estate: London 1998)

Chapter 1

For background on the art and theory of bridge building, see:

—*A Span of Bridges*, H. L. Hopkins (David and Charles: Newton Abbot 1970)

—*The Book of Bridges: The History, Technology and Romance of Bridges and their Builders*, Martin Hayden (Marshall Cavendish: London 1976)

—*The Tower and the Bridge: The New Art of Structural Engineering*, David P. Billington (Basic Books: New York 1983)

—*Bridges*, Peter Bishop (Reaktion Books: London 2008)

For the origins of London, the first bridges over the Thames and the life, times and mythology of Old London Bridge and the river, see:

—*London Bridge: 2,000 Years of a River Crossing*, Bruce Watson, Trevor Brigham and Tony Dyson (Museum of London: London 2001)

—'Roman London: Recent Finds and Research', A. Wardle and B. Watson (*Journal of Roman Archaeology*, November 1998)

—*Old London Bridge: Lost and Found*, Bruce Watson (Museum of London: London 2004)

—*Roman London*, Gordon Home (Benn: London 1926)

—*Medieval London*, Gordon Home (Benn: London 1927)

—*Old London Bridge*, Gordon Home (Bodley Head: London 1931)

—*Chronicles of London Bridge*, R. Thompson (London: 1827)

—*Old London Bridge: The Story of the Longest Inhabited Bridge in Europe*, Patricia Pierce (Review: London 2002)

—*Crossing London's River*, John Pudney (Dent: London 1972)

—*Liquid History: The Thames Through Time*, Stephen Croad (B. T. Batsford: London 2003)

—*Thames: Sacred River*, Peter Ackroyd (Vintage: London 2008)

—*The House by the Thames: And the People Who Lived There*, Gillian Tindall (Chatto & Windus: London 2006)

Also see:

—*London in Roman Times*, R. E. M. Wheeler (Lancaster House: London 1946)

—*Londinium: London in the Roman Empire*, John Morris, revised by Sarah Macready (Phoenix Giant: London 1999, 1982)

—*London: City of the Romans*, Ralph Merrifield (Batsford: London 1983)

—*Roman London*, Jenny Hall and Ralph Merrifield (Museum of London/ HMSO: London 1986)

—*The Anglo-Saxon Age: A Very Short Introduction*, John Blair (OUP: Oxford 2000)

—*Anglo-Saxon England*, F. M. Stenton (OUP: Oxford 2001)

—*Chaucer's London: Everyday life in London 1342–1400*, A. R. Myers (The History Press Ltd: Stroud 2009)

—*Medieval London: From Commune to Capital*, Gwyn A. Williams (Athlone Press: London 1963)

—*The Building of London from the Conquest to the Great Fire*, John Schofield (Museum of London: London 1984)

For the origins of the 'London Bridge is Falling Down' nursery rhyme, see the main London Bridge histories above and Chris Roberts' *Heavy Words Lightly Thrown: The Reason Behind the Rhyme* (Granta: London 2005) and *The Oxford Dictionary of Nursery Rhymes*, edited by Iona and Peter Opie (OUP: Oxford 1997). For more of Olaf's Saga see *Heimskringla*, translated by Samuel Laing, revised with an introduction and notes by Jacqueline Simpson (Dent: London; Dutton: New York, 1964).

The Rebuilding of London After the Great Fire, T. F. Reddaway (Jonathan Cape: London 1940) is a good place to start on London's redevelopment and eventual westward expansion post 1666, along with John Summerson's *Christopher Wren* (Collins: London 1951) and *Georgian London* (Barrie: London 1948, revised edition 1970) and Lisa Jardine's *On a Grander Scale: The Outstanding Career of Sir Christopher Wren* (HarperCollins: London 2002) and *The Curious Life of Robert Hooke: The Man who Measured London* (HarperCollins: London 2004), and *A More Beautiful City: Robert Hooke and the Rebuilding of London After the Great Fire*, Michael Cooper (The History Press Ltd: Stroud 2003)

Chapter 2

For material on Thomas Paine, see:

—*Tom Paine and Revolutionary America*, Eric Foner (OUP: Oxford 1977)
—*Tom Paine: The Life of a Revolutionary*, Harry Harmer (Haus: London 2006)
—*Thomas Paine: Enlightenment, Revolution, and the Birth of Modern Nations*, Craig Nelson (Profile: London 2007)
—*Tom Paine: A Political Life*, John Keane (Bloomsbury: London 1995)
—*Thomas Paine's Rights of Man: A Biography*, Christopher Hitchens (Atlantic: London 2006)

For Paine on his iron bridge, see:

—*The Writings of Thomas Paine – Volume IV*, collected and edited by Moncure Daniel Conway (G. P. Putnam's Sons: New York 1894)

For iron bridges, as well as Hopkins (1970), Hayden (1976), Billington (1983) and Bishop (2008), see:

—*The Iron Bridge: Symbol of the Industrial Revolution*, Barrie Trinder and Neil Cossons (Phillimore & Co. Ltd: Chichester 2002)

—*Iron Bridge: History and Guide*, Richard Hayman and Wendy Horton (The History Press Ltd: Stroud 2008)

—*Iron Bridge to Crystal Palace: Impact and Images of the Industrial Revolution*, Asa Briggs (Thames and Hudson: London 1979)

For the Wearmouth Bridge, see above and 'Thomas Wilson's Cast Iron Bridges 1800–1810', J. G. James (*Transactions of the Newcomen Society* 50, 1978–9)

Thomas Pennant's descriptions of London can be read in *Some account of London, Westminster and Southwark: illustrated with numerous views* (London: 1813)

For the development of the working river, see:

—*London's Docks*, John Pudney (Thames and Hudson: London 1975)

—*London Docks 1800–1980 : A Civil Engineering History*, Ivan S. Greeves (Telford Ltd: London 1980)

Chapter 3

For the rival designs for a new London Bridge, see the general London Bridge histories previously listed, but in particular Home (1931), Pudney

(1972) and Cookson (2006). Much of the more detailed information concerning the 'new' London Bridge, in this and in the following chapters, is drawn from the records and various notebooks held in the archives of the Institution of Civil Engineers.

For an account of Thomas Telford's rise to fortune, replete with practically Dickensian characters and turns of fate, see:
—*The Life of Thomas Telford, civil engineer*, Samuel Smiles (John Murray: London 1867)

For less morally improving biographical material and facts about Telford and his works see:
—*Thomas Telford*, L. T. C. Rolt (The History Press Ltd: Stroud 2007)
—*Thomas Telford*, Anthony Burton (Aurum Press Ltd: London 2000)

Both Billington (1983) and Hopkins (1970) consider his plans for London Bridge in some detail; the former is especially good on Telford's innovations with iron. A. W. Skempton's 'Telford and the designs for a new London Bridge' in *Thomas Telford: Engineer*, edited by Alistair Penfold (Telford Ltd: London 1980) provides the most thorough assessment of its probable technical merits and defects.

Chapter 4
For accounts of the Great Frost Fair 1814 see:
—*The Every-day Book: Or Everlasting Calendar of Popular Amusements, Sports*, William Hone (London, 1827)
—*Curiosities of London*, John Timbs (J. S. Virtue: London 1867)
—*Annals of London: A Year by Year Record of a Thousand Years Of History*, John Richardson (Weidenfeld & Nicolson: London 2001)

Though fiction, and based on an earlier freeze in 1608, Virginia Woolf's 1928 novel *Orlando* contains one of the most evocative descriptions of a Frost Fair on the Thames ever written.

For this further competition to design London Bridge, see sources for the previous chapter and again the records at the Institution of Civil Engineers and London Metropolitan Archives.

For John Rennie Snr, see Reyburn (1972) and:

—*Lives of the Engineers: Harbours – Lighthouses – Bridges; Smeaton and Rennie*, Samuel Smiles (John Murray: London 1874)

—*John Rennie, 1761–1821: The life and work of a great engineer*, C. T. G. Boucher (Manchester University Press: Manchester 1963)

—*Autobiography of Sir John Rennie*, Sir John Rennie (London 1875)

Bella Bathurst's *The Lighthouse Stevenson: the extraordinary story of the building of the Scottish lighthouses by the ancestors of Robert Louis Stevenson* (HarperCollins: London 1999) alludes briefly to the spat between Rennie and Stevenson over the Bell Rock Lighthouse.

The Duke of Wellington's commitment to the cause of a new London Bridge and his visits to the site during its construction are recalled by Sir John Rennie in his autobiography, where he also reminisces about his days at school with Shelley. The latter is also quoted by Richard Holmes in *Shelley: The Pursuit* (Quartet Books: London 1976).

Chapter 5

See the previously mentioned London Bridge histories for accounts of the opening ceremony, and for Mr Green's plans to balloon across the

Atlantic, see *The Dominion of the Air: The Story of Aerial Navigation*, Rev. J. M. Bacon (Cassell: London 1902).

For William IV's nautical airs and his time in New York during the Revolution, see:
—*The Life and Times of William IV*, Anne Somerset (Weidenfeld & Nicolson: London 1980)
—*King William IV*, Philip Ziegler (Cassell: London 1989)
—*Sailor King: The Life of King William IV*, Tom Pocock (Sinclair-Stevenson: London 1991)

For the dispersal of material from Old London Bridge see again previous London Bridge histories but especially Watson, Brigham and Dyson (2001) and Home (1931). The former contains the best information on what went where, with a few photographs of the existing material to boot.

Chapter 6

The London That Nobody Knows, directed by Norman Cohen (1967), was loosely adapted by Brian Comport from Geoffrey Fletcher's book of the same title (Hutchinson: London 1962). Bob Stanley's fine survey of the film was entitled 'The Naked City', and appeared in the *Guardian*, 21 November 2003.

Ian Nairn's guide to the capital's architecture during this period was *Nairn's London* (Penguin: Harmondsworth 1966). For Fletcher on the proposal for a new London Bridge, see *London River* (Hutchinson: London 1966).

Joe Moran credits W. H. Auden with the first use of the term 'commuter' in print in Britain in *Queuing for Beginners* (Profile: London 2008), but his excellent *On Roads* (Profile: London 2010) also contains much that is germane to this chapter as a whole.

See *Festival of Britain*, edited by Elaine Harwood and Alan Powers (Twentieth Century Society: London 2001) for material on the legacy of the 1951 jamboree on the South Bank.

Alison Smithson's comments on consumerism are taken from the monograph *Alison and Peter Smithson: from a House of the Future to a House of Today*, edited by Dirk van den Heuvel and Max Risselada (010 Publications/Design Museum: London 2004).

For the transformation of Britain's cities after the war and into the 1960s also see:
—*Brutalism: Post-War British Architecture*, Alexander Clement (Crowood Press: Marlborough 2011)
—*Militant Modernism*, Owen Hatherley (Zero Books: London 2009)
—*Building the Post-War World*, Nicholas Bullock (Routledge: London 2002)
—*Town Planning in Britain Since 1900: The Rise and Fall of the Planning Ideal*, Gordon E. Cherry (Wiley-Blackwell: Oxford 1996)
—*A Broken Wave: The Rebuilding of England, 1940–1980*, Lionel Esher (Allen Lane: London 1981)
—*Architectural Review* May 1962, 'Traffic in Towns', Colin Buchanan (Penguin/HMSO: London 1964)
—*London 2000*, Peter Hall (Faber & Faber: London 1963)
—*Motopia: a study in the evolution of urban landscape*, G. A. Jellicoe (Studio Books: London 1961)

For Robert Moses in the States, see:

—*All That is Solid Melts into Air: The Experience of Modernity*, Marshall Berman (Penguin: London 1988)

—*The Death and Life of Great American Cities*, Jane Jacobs (Penguin: London 1965)

—*Wrestling with Moses: How Jane Jacobs Took on New York's Master Builder and Transformed the American City*, Anthony Flint (Random House: New York 2011)

Back issues of *Guildhall*, the Corporation of London's newsletter, cover the period of the new bridge's development and the sale of the old one, and can be perused in the London Metropolitan Archives.

For William Holford, see *Holford: a study in architecture, planning and civic design*, Gordon E. Cherry and Leith Penny (Mansell: London 1986) and again Esher (1981). Both include thorough accounts of the Paternoster Square development and his unrealised schemes for Piccadilly Circus.

Robert Finch's dismissal of Holford's Paternoster Square as 'ghastly', etc., was taken from 'Wonders and blunders', *Guardian*, 24 May 2004.

For the seamier side of Piccadilly Circus, see *Capital Affairs: The Making of the Permissive Society*, Frank Mort (Yale University Press: New Haven, CT 2009) and *London Calling*, Barry Miles (Atlantic Books: London 2010). The Kenneth Williams quote is from *The Kenneth Williams Diaries*, edited by Russell Davies (HarperCollins: London 1993).

Chapter 7

For Ivan Luckin, see Johnson (1981) and Malach (1981) again, and Grelle White's interview with Luckin, 'How London Bridge was sold to the States', *Watford Observer*, 6 May 1983 (republished online under *This is Local London* banner, 27 March 2002). Luckin's own papers and various other cuttings and the relevant press releases about the sale are held in the London Metropolitan Archives in Clerkenwell. Some of the best anecdotes about Luckin came from my interview on 1 November 2010 with Archie Galloway OBE, whose father had been at school with Luckin and also held a seat on the Corporation of London's Common Council from 1981 to 2009. Galloway was not only generous with his time and memories of Luckin but also shared his own researches into the sale of London Bridge and his paper 'Ivan Luckin and the sale of London Bridge', presented to the Guildhall Historical Association on 16 June 2008.

For William Randolph Hearst see:

—*Citizen Hearst: A biography of William Randolph Hearst*, William Swanberg (Bantam Books: New York 1963)
—*The Chief: The life of William Randolph Hearst*, David Nasaw (Gibson Square: London 2002)
—*William Randolph Hearst: Final edition, 1911–1951*, Ben Procter (OUP: Oxford 2007)
—*Hearst Castle, San Simeon*, Thomas R. Aidala with photographs by Curtis Bruce (Hudson Hills: New York 1981)

P. G. Wodehouse's account of visiting Hearst's 'ranch' can be found in *Performing Flea: A Self-Portrait in Letters*, P. G. Wodehouse, edited by W. Townend (Penguin Books: Harmondsworth 1961).

Tom Wolfe's arguments about vulgar American tourists are quoted in *We'll Always Have Paris: American Tourists in France since 1930*, Harvey Levenstein (University Of Chicago Press: Chicago 2004).

For the destruction of the Euston Propylaeum and the Coal Exchange see:

—'The Euston Murder', J. M. Richards, *Architectural Review* April 1962
—*The Euston Arch and the growth of the London, Midland and Scottish Railway*, Alison and Peter Smithson (Thames & Hudson: London 1968)
—'Raise the Euston Arch', Jonathan Glancey, *Guardian*, 15 March 2010
—*Saving a Century* (The Victorian Society: London 2010)

Also see:

—*Stylistic Cold Wars: Betjeman Versus Pevsner*, Timothy Mowl (John Murray: London 2000)
—*John Betjeman: The Biography*, Bevis Hillier (John Murray: London 2006)
—*Nikolaus Pevsner: The Life*, Susie Harries (Chatto & Windus: London 2011)

Derek Jarman's reflections on this era appear in *Modern Nature: The journals of Derek Jarman* (Century: London 1991)

Chapter 8

All press releases and so on quoted from here are held in the London Metropolitan Archives, and as per previous chapter. John Crosby's 'Swinging London' piece 'London – The Most Exciting City' appeared in the *Sunday Telegraph* on 16 April 1965 and *Time*'s 'London: The Swinging City' was 15 April 1966. Also see *Ready, Steady, Go!: Swinging*

London and the Invention of Cool, Shawn Levy (Fourth Estate: London 2002) and the George Melly-scripted satire, *Smashing Time* (1967). Melly on Sarne et al. is from his *Revolt into Style: The Pop Arts in Britain* (Penguin: Harmondsworth 1972).

For Sir Patrick Dean, see obituaries by Alan Campbell, *Independent*, 8 November 1994 and Eric Pace, *New York Times*, 16 November 1994.

For the British government's dealings with President Johnson in general see *A Special Relationship: Anglo-American Relations from the Cold War to Iraq*, John Dumbrell (Palgrave Macmillan: London 2006).

Chapter 9

For C. V. Wood, see Johnson (1981) and Malach (1981) again, and 'C. V. Wood Jnr, Who Pioneered Large Theme Parks, Is Dead at 71', Bruce Lambert, *New York Times*, 16 March 1992. For more on his theme-park work, see *Walt Disney: The Biography*, Neal Gabler (Alfred A. Knopf: New York 2006) and 'Celebrating the Short, Sweet Ride of Freedomland', David Gonzalez, City Room, *New York Times*, 19 June 2010.

For Chasen's restaurant see 'Memories Taste Like This', Lora Zarubin, *Los Angeles Times* Magazine, 12 March 2010 and 'Chasen's Chili Is History as Once Star-Studded Eatery Closes', Staff Reporter, *Los Angeles Times*, 2 April 1995.

For Robert Paxton McCulloch, the creation of Lake Havasu City and the purchase of London Bridge, see again Judson Frost (1987), Johnson (1981) and Malach (1981).

For Hedgepeth's observations on the mobility of Americans and a contemporary account of late 1960s' utopianism, see *The Alternative: Communal Life in New America*, William Hedgepeth and Dennis Stock (Macmillan: New York 1970). Also see *Droppers: America's first hippie commune, Drop City*, Mark Matthews (University of Oklahoma Press: Oklahoma 2010), and in fiction *Drop City*, T. C. Boyle (Bloomsbury: London 2003)

For Eisenhower, see:
— *Eisenhower*, Geoffrey Perret (Random House: New York 1999)
— *Eisenhower*, Peter G. Boyle (Pearson/Longman: Harlow 2005)
— *Eisenhower: Soldier and President*, Stephen E. Ambrose (Simon and Schuster: London/New York 1991).

Also see *The Lost Continent: Travels in Small Town America*, Bill Bryson (Secker & Warburg: London 1992) for Bryson's withering take on Ike's reading habits.

Bryce's views on the west are quoted in *The Significance of the Frontier in American History*, Frederick Jackson Turner (Penguin: London 2008). Also worth consulting in regard to the 'pioneering' spirit of America is *The Future of Nostalgia*, Svetlana Boym (Basic Books: New York 2001), in which she argues that early nineteenth-century Americans perceived themselves as 'Nature's Nation' – a people who lived in the present and had 'no need of the past'. 'American youthful forgetfulness', she writes at one point, 'allowed for the nationalization of progress and the creation of another quasi-metaphysical entity called the American way of life.'

R. E. M. Wheeler's view about London being a parasite of London Bridge is expressed in *London in Roman Times* (London Museum: London 1930)

Counter-intuitive as it might at first sound, the film releases cited here were gleaned from reviews in that week's issue of the *Listener* magazine.

Chapter 10

For Arthur Furguson, see:

—*Brewer's Rogues, Villains and Eccentrics*, William Donaldson (Phoenix: London 2004)

—*The Man Who Sold Nelson's Column, and other Scottish frauds and hoaxes*, Dane Love (Birlinn: Edinburgh 2007)

—'TV quiz host Stephen Fry duped by story of fictional Scots conman', Raymond Hainey, *Sunday Mail*, 8 February 2008

For the other monument vendors and swindlers mentioned, see:

—*The Man Who sold the Eiffel Tower*, J. F. Johnson and F. Miller (W. H. Allen: London 1962)

—*The Deceivers: Lives of Great Imposters*, Egon Larsen (Roy: New York 1966)

—*History's Greatest Deceptions, and the People Who Planned Them*, Eric Chaline (The History Press Ltd: Stroud 2010)

—'For You, Half Price' Gabriel Cohen, *New York Times*, 27 November 2005

For Tower Bridge's prospects after the 1960s, see Pudney (1972). For C.V. Wood's alleged confession, see 'Bridge Across the Atlantic', Nigel Williamson, *Independent*, 13 September 1997. My account of the newspaper conference was taken from my interview with Stanley Usinowicz in Lake Havasu City on 27 September 2011. Williamson also interviewed Usinowicz for his article, though reached a rather different conclusion from quite similar pieces of information.

Chapter 11

The Spectrum's adventures in antique dealing can be enjoyed in the 6 January 1968 issue of the *Lady Penelope* comic.

For the bridge stone-shipping and rebuilding and opening, see the main London Bridge histories but especially Johnson (1981), Malach (1981) and Reyburn (1972).

For the confusion over Sir Peter Studd's hotel booking, see his obituary, *Daily Telegraph*, 30 June 2003.

Chapter 12

For McCulloch's demise and the break-up of his business empire, see:

—'Land Concern Plead Guilty to 19 Counts of Criminal Fraud: McCulloch Properties, in a Colorado Court Pact, Agrees to Pay About $16 Million in Cash and Land', Grace Lichtenstein, *New York Times*, 23 February 1977

—'New Finding in McCulloch Death', Grace Lichtenstein, *New York Times*, 27 February 1977

—'The Man Who Won McCulloch Oil', Pamela G. Hollie, *New York Times*, 13 July 1980

For the comment about MAXXAM and Rush Limbaugh, see 'Market Place: The investor Charles Hurwitz may be clearing up some feuds', Allen R. Myerson, *New York Times*, 14 July 1994.